The United States Congress

MANCHESTER
UNIVERSITY PRESS

Ross M. English

The United States Congress

Manchester University Press

Manchester and New York

distributed exclusively in the USA by Palgrave

Published by Manchester University Press
Oxford Road, Manchester M13 9NR, UK
and Room 400, 175 Fifth Avenue, New York, NY 10010, USA
www.manchesteruniversitypress.co.uk

Distributed exclusively in the USA by
Palgrave, 175 Fifth Avenue, New York,
NY 10010, USA

Distributed exclusively in Canada by
UBC Press, University of British Columbia, 2029 West Mall,
Vancouver, BC, Canada V6T 1Z2

British Library Cataloguing-in-Publication Data
A catalogue record for this book is available from the British Library

Library of Congress Cataloging-in-Publication Data applied for

ISBN 0 7190 6308 6 *hardback*
     0 7190 6309 4 *paperback*

First published 2003

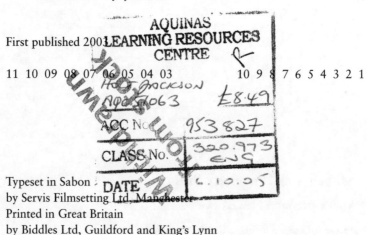

11 10 09 08 07 06 05 04 03   10 9 8 7 6 5 4 3 2 1

Typeset in Sabon
by Servis Filmsetting Ltd, Manchester
Printed in Great Britain
by Biddles Ltd, Guildford and King's Lynn

To my parents,
Len and Cynthia English

Contents

List of tables and boxes   *page* viii

Preface   ix

1 Origins and development of Congress   1

2 Congressional elections   16

3 Representatives and Senators   39

4 The committee system   61

5 Parties in Congress   87

6 Floor deliberations and beyond   105

7 President and Congress   120

8 Congress, the media and interest groups   143

9 Assessing the US Congress   160

   Select bibliography   170

   Index   173

List of tables and boxes

Tables

2.1 Party control of the House and Senate since
1945   *page* 18
2.2 Party identification 3-point scale 1952–98   23
2.3a The coat-tails effect?   33
2.3b Mid-term election performance of the
President's party   34
7.1 Presidential vetoes   134

Boxes

1.1 John Locke and the social contract   5
2.1 Jon Corzine v. Bob Franks, New Jersey Senate
2000   28
3.1 Previous occupations of members of the 106th
Congress   41
4.1 Congressional committees   64
4.2 Classification of committees   72
4.3 The battle for campaign finance   81
5.1 Party leadership in the 107th Congress   89
6.1 An example of a rule   108

Preface

The United States Congress is one of the world's most powerful legislatures. It is a complex, but often fascinating, institution. It is a place of contrasts, where most of the day-to-day work is mundane and unremarkable but can occasionally provide moments of great drama. To read the history of Congress is to learn about both the great and infamous names and moments of American politics.

The aim of this book is to provide an introduction to the US Congress. It makes no claims to formulate any new theories or models of Congressional action. What it attempts to do is explain the role of Congress and its internal procedures. Particular issues and examples are highlighted to try and give the reader an understanding of some of the complexities and nuances of the legislative process in the United States.

One of the difficulties in writing a text such as this is that politics does not ever stand still. Events constantly threaten to usurp the information written here. Indeed, this fact was behind the inception of this book. The 1994 election gave the Republican Party control of Congress for the first time in forty years and ushered in a period of rapid change. Textbooks written before 1994, through no fault of their own, were in danger of becoming outdated. Consequently, much of the material in this text focuses on events since that time.

I would like to thank all those who have helped to bring this project to fruition: Professor Chris Bailey for sparking my interest in the US Congress; all the staff and students in the Department of Politics and International Relations at the University of Reading for their support; Alan Cromartie for assistance with John Locke; all members of the American Politics Group of the Political Science Association; Jon Herbert for his help with my Reagan queries; the anonymous reviewers whose comments proved valuable in shaping the final product; all at Manchester University Press for their hard work; and, finally, to my partner Clare for her unfailing support.

1

Origins and development of Congress

All legislative Powers herein granted shall be vested in a Congress of the United States, which shall consist of a Senate and House of Representatives. (The Constitution of the United States of America, Article 1, Section 1)

The origins of the Constitution

In 1787, when the Founding Fathers of the United States of America crafted the Constitution – a Constitution which still endures today – they chose for the very first article, not the institution of the President or the Supreme Court, but the US Congress. The Constitution gave Congress the power to make laws for the federal government, the ability to check the actions of the President and the responsibility of representing the American people.

Constitutions are never written in a vacuum. They reflect the beliefs, goals and ambitions of their authors, and in many cases, the values of society. In this way the American Constitution is no exception. What is exceptional about the document, which British Prime Minister William Gladstone once described as 'the most wonderful work ever struck off at a given time by the brain and purpose of man', is that over 200 years after its conception it still forms the basis of the government of the United States. Consequently, to be able to understand the principles on which the US Congress was founded, one must first understand the politics which surrounded the formation of the United States of America.

The founding of British colonies in what was known as the 'new world' is only one part of the history of the Americas, but it is central to the history of the United States. It was from the British colonies that, in 1776, a new nation was born.

The first British colonists arrived in what is now Virginia in 1585. Life was difficult in the new world and many of the early colonies succumbed to disease, famine and attack by indigenous 'Indian' tribes. The first colony to overcome these difficulties and survive was established in Jamestown, Virginia in 1607. Their success was due to two factors: surviving the first winter with the aid of friendly Native Americans and an ability to grow tobacco. The colonists had discovered a mix of Caribbean and mainland American tobacco leaves which was appealing to the European palate and trade with the 'old world' had become both possible and profitable. By 1732, thirteen colonies had been established up and down the eastern seaboard of North America. These colonies began to thrive through trade and soon found a degree of autonomy from the British Government (throughout this time Britain had been more concerned with the aftermath of its own civil war than with the affairs of the colonists in the West). Colonial assemblies were established in America and these began to check the power of the resident royal governors, often taking control of aspects of taxation and expenditure. Gradually, the principles of self-government were becoming established in the minds of the colonists.

As the eighteenth century progressed, the British Crown and Parliament once again began to look to the West. The colonies had proved to be a success and Britain wanted to expand their control of the continent. Their attempts at westward expansion, however, meant conflict with French forces who had established a powerful position in North America. The 'French Indian War' lasted from 1754 to 1763, until defeat for the French forces left the British in control of a large area of what is now Canada and the United States. The cost of the war and the resources needed to control their newly expanded western empire put a strain on British finances and led Parliament to look for new ways to raise revenue. Having decided that the colonies should pay more for their own defence, the British Parliament passed a series of Acts which levied taxes on colonial trade. Two taxes caused particular resentment among the colonists. The Sugar Act of 1764 banned the import of rum, placed a duty on molasses imported from non-English areas and introduced taxes on wines, silks, coffee and other luxury items. A year later, the Stamp Act taxed all newspapers, pamphlets, licenses, leases and other legal documents, a measure which affected anyone who did business. Other initiatives introduced by the British included a ban on credit notes and a requirement that the colonies provide royal troops with provisions and barracks.

The British actions had threatened the ability of the colonies to trade freely and, given the historical importance of trade to the colonies' existence, caused a great deal of resentment. Central to the complaint was the fact that the colonies had no representation in Parliament – the body that had instigated the taxes which had provoked the conflict. A call for 'no taxation without representation' lay at the heart of their grievances. Over the next ten years protests over British taxation and coercion grew, occasionally breaking into violence. Matters came to a head in Lexington, Massachusetts in 1775 when a raid by British troops on colonial militias led to full-scale fighting and the start of the American Revolution.

A formal Declaration of Independence was issued on 4 July 1776. Largely written by Thomas Jefferson of Virginia, the Declaration set out the grounds on which the colonies claimed their right to throw off British rule. They charged that the history of King George III's rule was

> a history of repeated injuries and usurpations, all having in direct object the establishment of an absolute Tyranny over these States . . . In every stage of these Oppressions We have Petitioned for Redress in the most humble terms: Our repeated Petitions have been answered only by repeated injury. A Prince whose character is thus marked by every act which may define a Tyrant, is unfit to be the ruler of a free people.

Behind the Declaration were the ideas of eighteenth-century philosophers and writers such as Thomas Paine and John Locke, which were prevalent among the aristocracy of the time. Particularly influential was Locke's *social contract theory* (see Box 1.1). These ideas would go on to play a large part in the writing of the Constitution.

The War of Independence formally ended in 1783 with the signing of the Treaty of Paris in which the British Crown acknowledged the independence, freedom and sovereignty of the thirteen former colonies. With victory assured, the thirteen states were faced with the task of devising a system of government. Having just defeated what they viewed as a despotic power, the leaders of the new states had no intention of replacing the British Crown with their own monarch or creating a central government with the power to deny any state its rights ever again. However, it was recognised that some form of central administration was inevitable if the new indepen-

Box 1.1   John Locke and the social contract

Seventeenth-century philosopher John Locke was one of the key architects of the social contract theory. Locke argued that governments were formed with the consent of its citizens. The people agreed to obey the government (thus surrendering some of their freedom to act as they choose) on the understanding that government would use its power to protect their natural rights of 'lives, liberties and estates'. The power of the individual to enforce the 'laws of nature' by administering punishments on those who broke them (up to and including the death penalty) was surrendered to the government. On the other side of the contract, if the government broke its promise and failed to respect the basic rights of the citizenry, it lost its own legitimacy and could be overthrown by the people.

It was partly on this basis that the Declaration of Independence stated that the British Crown had, through abusing the rights of the American colonists, forfeited its right to govern. It was then the duty of the American people to rise up against their British rulers and to institute their own government. This task was completed with American victory in the War of Independence.

dent states were to succeed. The result was the *Articles of Confederation*, drawn up in 1776, adopted in 1777, and which came into effect in 1781.

Articles of Confederation

Driven by an unwillingness by the states to relinquish their independence to a strong central power for fear of abuses, the Articles of Confederation created a central government with very little power. There was to be no president or head of state and no judiciary. The only national body was a *unicameral* (having only one chamber) Congress, made up of delegates from the thirteen states. The Congress was responsible for conducting foreign affairs, declaring war and peace, maintaining an army and navy and a variety of other lesser functions. But the Articles denied Congress the power to collect taxes, regulate interstate commerce or enforce laws.

The new system proved unworkable. Suffering financially from the effect of the war, the economies of the states were in trouble, with farmers hit particularly hard. Trade disputes grew between various states, exacerbated by the fact that no standard national currency had been established. Protests sprung up across America, with some descending into violence. The tensions between states was not calmed by the fact that nine states had organised their own armies, and in some cases, navies as well.

It was soon recognised that a stronger national government had become necessary to ensure the peaceful survival of the states. To this end the leaders of the states met at the Federal Convention in the Philadelphia State House in May 1787. The initial purpose was to amend the Articles of Confederation, but before long the leaders had agreed that an entirely new system was needed. On 17 September 1787, after sixteen weeks of deliberation, thirty-nine of the forty-two delegates put their signature to the new Constitution of the United States of America. Two years later the document had been ratified by the required number of states and the first Congress of the United States of America convened in New York City.

The Constitution of the United States

Although the Constitution established a central government with far more authority than the one created under the

Articles of Confederation, this did not mean the states had overcome their fear of despotism. The system of government laid out in the Constitution was deliberately designed to prevent any abuse of the rights of the states. It did this by creating a *federal* system based on the principle of *separation of powers*

Federalism

There was never a question that the new United States of America would be anything other than federal. A federal state maintains more than one level of government, with each having their own rights and independence. Unlike in Britain, where the government in London is pre-eminent, and can create, alter or abolish local governments as it sees fit, the new US Constitution maintained the autonomy of the individual states. They created a central, or federal, government with certain powers and responsibilities out of necessity. As the failure of the Articles of Confederation showed, there were certain jobs, necessary for the success of the new nation, that could not be carried out by the state governments alone. However, under the new Constitution, the state governments were intended to be the primary level of government, with responsibility for their own affairs and those of their citizens. The federal government was to be restricted to those areas which fell outside of the individual state: regulating trade between states, establishing a national currency, conducting foreign affairs and controlling the national military forces. This ideal where each level of government had its own distinct areas of influence which did not cross was known as *dual federalism*. As we will see, such a pure form of federalism was going to be short lived, but for the early years of the United States it was the state governments which held the power.

Separation of powers

The Founding Fathers were aware that, whatever their intentions, without some form of safeguard, the powers given to the federal government could be abused. To counter such an eventuality, a system of checks and balances within the federal government itself was established. Rather than invest one body or person with full responsibility for the running of the government, the powers were separated out between three distinct and separate bodies: the executive, the legislature and the judiciary. In principle, no decision could be taken without the possibility that it could be checked by one of the other bodies.

Congress in the Constitution

Just as the Constitution established a system whereby each branch of government would be checked by another, a bicameral legislature was chosen so Congress could in effect act as a check upon itself. For any law to be passed the consent of both chambers would be needed. These two chambers which make up the US Congress were, and are, the *House of Representatives* and the *Senate*.

House of Representatives

One of the central complaints against the former British rulers was that Parliament taxed the people of the colonies but allowed them no representation in the body where such decisions were made. In order to avoid repeating such a wrong in the new United States, the citizens of the states were granted representation in the House of Representatives. Representatives were to be directly elected by popular vote every two years. This short time between elections was to ensure that Representatives would remain sensitive to the wishes of their electorate, or face a swift removal. The number of Representatives returned from each state was determined by the size of the state's population.

While the creation of a directly elected chamber in the national legislature was a radical development for the late eighteenth century, this was no modern-style democracy. Voting rights were limited to white male adults, and in some states a property qualification was also added. Furthermore, the House of Representatives would also have to work together, and in some cases compete, with the other chamber of Congress, the US Senate.

Senate

The creation of the Senate can be viewed as a response to two of the Founding Fathers' concerns. The first was that if left unchecked, the popular House may make rash and unwise decisions. While the people deserved representation, there was a concern that the masses could be swayed into supporting candidates or policies which were not necessarily in the best interests of the United States. There was a danger that such regular elections may lead to the House pursuing short-term policies. Secondly, there was a fear that with the number of Representatives from each state determined by population, a few larger states could ride roughshod over the wishes of the rest of the House.

To meet these concerns the Senate was designed to be the chamber which represented the states. Each state was given equal representation, returning two Senators, each representing the whole state, regardless of size of population. While the House, with its regular elections, was intended to be responsive to the current concerns of the population, Senators were to serve for six-year terms. The length of tenure was designed to allow the Senate to take a longer term view when making their decisions. In addition to this, under the original Constitution, Senators were not subject to election by the voters of each state; rather they were to be appointed by the legislature of their respective states. Free from having to please the masses and with their extended terms of office, the Founding Fathers hoped that the Senate would act as a more sober body, checking any unwise or impetuous proposals which emerged from the House. This situation lasted until 1913 when the Constitution was amended to provide for the direct election of Senators.

Congressional powers and responsibilities

Legislation

The primary power and responsibility of Congress is that of legislation. Congress has the sole legislative power; no other body in the United States can make federal legislation (state legislatures can, of course, make legislation for their own state). Bills can only be introduced into Congress by a Representative or Senator, although for the most part a bill can originate in either chamber. For any bill to become law it must pass a majority vote of both the House and Senate.

While Congress possesses sole legislative power, it is subject to the checks and balances written into the Constitution. Once a bill has passed Congress, it must then be sent to the President for his[1] approval. The President has ten days (excluding Sundays) to exercise one of three options. He can sign the bill into law, he can do nothing allowing (after the ten days) the bill to pass into law without his approval, or he can veto the bill which returns the legislation to Congress preventing it

becoming law. However, because Congress is the final authority when it comes to legislation, a presidential veto does not
end matters. Congress has the power to override a veto if (and
it is often a big *if*) a two-thirds majority can be obtained in a
vote in *both* the House and Senate. If this majority is achieved,
the bill will become law despite the objections of the President.

Oversight

As part of the system of checks and balances, Congress has the
power and responsibility to police many of the actions of the
executive. While both chambers have a role to play here, it is
the Senate which was given the bulk of the responsibility. All
presidential appointments, whether they be to the courts,
ambassadorships or to the cabinet must be approved by the
Senate. Treaties signed by the President only come into effect
once ratified by a two-thirds majority of the Senate. While the
President is Commander-in-Chief of the Armed Forces, Congress controls the funds needed to run the forces and only the
House of Representatives can declare war. As we shall see later,
some of these checks proved to be more effective than others.

Congress constantly monitors the behaviour of the executive branch, something which will be examined further in
chapter 7. For extreme cases, the Constitution awarded Congress with the ultimate power – the power to remove the
President from office. The House of Representatives was
given the power of impeachment if the President is guilty of
the ambiguous charge of 'high crimes and misdemeanours'.
Impeachment, though, does not mean removal from office.
That power was reserved for the Senate which, following
impeachment by the House, must then try the President for
his crimes, and if a two-thirds majority is reached, remove
him from office.

The development of Congress

The basic structures and principles of Congress at the beginning of the twenty-first century are the same as they were at the end of the eighteenth. The nation of the United States of America, however, has changed dramatically and the federal government has had to adapt to keep pace with these changes.

The Constitution has been amended only twenty-six times since its adoption, and in fact has changed very little. The first ten amendments, known as the 'Bill of Rights' were adopted in 1791 to satisfy state fears that their rights and those of their citizens were not sufficiently protected from abuses by the federal government. These rights included provisions concerning freedom of speech, freedom of association and the right to a fair trial, among others.

Gradually the right to vote was extended throughout the nineteenth and twentieth centuries. Non-white Americans were given the Constitutional right to vote in 1870, women gained equality in this regard in 1920 and the franchise was extended to 18-year-olds in 1971. The seventeenth amendment, ratified in 1913, provided for the direct election of Senators.

Many of the changes which have occurred in Congress have not appeared as Constitutional amendments. The role of Congress both in relation to its place in the federal government and within the nation as a whole has changed. The House and Senate have developed separate identities and styles, partly due to the different roles accorded them by the Constitution, and partly due to traditions which have developed over the years.

Congress currently resides in the Capitol Building on Capitol Hill, Washington DC, connected to the White House by Pennsylvania Avenue. It first moved to the nation's current capital in 1800, having spent the previous decade in Philadelphia. The building is now surrounded by offices for the Representatives, Senators and their staff and by the Library of Congress. All buildings are connected by a series of underground tunnels and are accessible by any member of public, provided they can pass thorough a security check. In this regard, the United States has one of the most open governments in the world today.

The balance of power within the federal government remained firmly tilted towards Congress throughout the nineteenth century and for the first half of the twentieth. Congress proudly protected its role as the sole source of legislation and resisted any attempts by the presidency to establish legislative leadership. The presidency had quickly established itself in a strong position in regards to foreign policy, but Congress played the dominant role in the areas of domestic policy played by the federal government.

Presidents Theodore Roosevelt (served 1901–09) and Woodrow Wilson (1913–21), the so-called 'progressive Presidents', both attempted to extend the influence of the presidency to areas of domestic policy, particularly the area of business monopolies. Both were unsuccessful as Congress spurned what it saw as an intrusion into its Constitutional role. The whole balance of power changed in 1932 with the election of Franklin Delano Roosevelt to the presidency. President Roosevelt came to the presidency at a time when the United States was suffering from a crippling economic depression. He was elected on a promise to use the federal government to address the problems faced by America. His 'New Deal' programme did much to help the nation out of its problems, but its effect on the political process would be even greater.

Roosevelt transformed the role of both the presidency and the federal government. Under his leadership the federal government became involved in areas such as welfare, employment and public works which were previously viewed as the preserve of the states. What was also notable was that many of these initiatives came not from Congress, but from the White House. Congress remained the only body with the power to pass legislation, but Roosevelt gave the presidency a leading role in formulating legislation for Congress to consider. Since Roosevelt's time, the President has regularly been an active participant in the legislative process.

While Congress was forced to adapt to the political changes in the late twentieth century, its role remains essentially the same. The extension of the federal government into areas previously reserved for state government has meant that the range of issues Congress must consider has increased dramatically as has the sheer complexity of the legislation it must pass. With the post-New Deal presidency looking to play a more active role in the initiation of legislation, the legislative process became increasingly characterised by co-operation and competition between Congress and the White House.

The balance of power between Congress and the presidency is constantly changing. Until the mid-1970s, academics often wrote of an 'imperial' presidency, which placed the executive as the dominant branch of government, especially in matters of foreign policy. With the failure of the war in Vietnam and the resignation of President Nixon following the Watergate scandal, both of which highlighted abuses of power by the White House, Congress began to reassert its power not only to check the presidency, but also in terms of its legislative role. Today the struggle for dominance over the direction of the federal government is a much more dynamic one.

Conclusion

The primary role of Congress in the American political system remains the same as when the Founding Fathers wrote the Constitution in 1787; all legislative power is still vested in a Congress of the United States, which consists of a Senate and House of Representatives. What has changed is the political and social context within which it operates. The latest change which Congress has had to adapt to came in 1994 when, in the mid-term election, the voters chose to elect a Republican majority in both the House of Representatives and the Senate for the first time since 1955. The following chapters aim to give an understanding of how Congress operates, both internally and within the wider political system. As part of this task, events since 1994 will play a prominent part in the explanation to show how Congress has adapted to the latest developments in American politics.

Notes

1 Masculine pronouns are used for convenience of style and are not intended to exclude females.

2

Congressional elections

All politics is local. (former House Speaker Tip O'Neil)

The Contract with America

In 1994 the Republican Party led by Newt Gingrich of Georgia in the House and future presidential candidate Bob Dole of Kansas in the Senate celebrated a remarkable victory in the Congressional elections. For the first time since 1955 the Republicans had gained a majority in both chambers of Congress. Indeed it was the first time in that forty-year period that the party had held the House of Representatives at all (see Table 2.1).

Newt Gingrich took much of the credit for the victory. Gingrich was an outspoken conservative who had risen quickly to a position of leadership within the Republican members of the House of Representatives. He was also the central figure behind the *Contract with America*. The *Contract* was a manifesto outlining ten key policies which, if a Republican majority were elected, would be brought to the floor of the House for a vote within the first 100 days. It was signed by a significant majority of Republican candidates standing in the House elections and many in the Republican

Party believed that this document was central to their success in the 1994 elections. It was the first time that so many of the candidates of one party had pledged themselves to a national platform of specific policies which, they argued, offered a sharp contrast to the ability of the previous Democrat Congress to get things done. As we shall see, there is evidence to suggest that they were mistaken in this belief.

Congressional elections

Elections to Congress are held every two years on the first Tuesday of November, electing the whole of the House and approximately one-third of the Senate each time. House members are elected from constituencies within states containing, on average, around 500,000 voters; Senators represent their entire state. The newly elected members take their seats at the start of the new Congress in January of the following year. In this way while the elections are always held in even-numbered years, each Congress begins and ends in the odd-numbered years.

What made the *Contract with America* in 1994 such a notable event in the history of Congressional elections is that conventional wisdom considers that local rather than national factors play the greater role in American election campaigns. Voters are assumed to vote as much on the achievements and character of the candidates before them as along a party line. Consequently, candidates run campaigns which stress their personal strengths or their opponent's weaknesses rather than the strengths and weaknesses of the respective parties. Campaign posters ask the public to 'Vote Gingrich' or 'Vote Gephardt' rather than 'Vote Republican' or 'Vote Democrat'. This phenomenon is known as *candidate-*

Table 2.1   Party control of the House and Senate since 1945

Congress	Year	House	Senate
79th	1945–47	Democrat	Democrat
80th	1947–49	*Republican*	*Republican*
81st	1949–51	Democrat	Democrat
82nd	1951–53	Democrat	Democrat
83rd	1953–55	*Republican*	*Republican*
84th	1955–57	Democrat	Democrat
85th	1957–59	Democrat	Democrat
86th	1959–61	Democrat	Democrat
87th	1961–63	Democrat	Democrat
88th	1963–65	Democrat	Democrat
89th	1965–67	Democrat	Democrat
90th	1967–69	Democrat	Democrat
91st	1969–71	Democrat	Democrat
92nd	1971–73	Democrat	Democrat
93rd	1973–75	Democrat	Democrat
94th	1975–77	Democrat	Democrat
95th	1977–79	Democrat	Democrat
96th	1979–81	Democrat	Democrat
97th	1981–83	Democrat	*Republican*
98th	1983–85	Democrat	*Republican*
99th	1985–87	Democrat	*Republican*
100th	1987–89	Democrat	Democrat
101st	1989–91	Democrat	Democrat
102nd	1991–93	Democrat	Democrat
103rd	1993–95	Democrat	Democrat
104th	1995–97	*Republican*	*Republican*
105th	1997–99	*Republican*	*Republican*
106th	1999–2001	*Republican*	*Republican*
107th	2001–03	*Republican*	Democrat*

* The 2000 election returned 50 Democrats and 50 Republicans to the
Senate, giving the Republicans control of the chamber thanks to the
casting vote of Vice-President Cheney. However, in May 2001, Senator
Jim Jeffords left the Republicans to become an independent, giving the
Democrats control of the Senate.

centred campaigning. It can be attributed to three character-istics of the American system.

Weak parties

Compared to the more dominant parties prevalent in Western Europe, American parties appear to be loose ideological groupings of legislators. As will be seen in chapter 5, party leaders in Congress and elsewhere attempt to persuade and cajole their members into voting along party lines. However, they have few sanctions available to force members of Congress to follow a fixed position. Such power would, in fact, be largely undesirable to the parties as they need to allow members the flexibility to act in the way most likely to lead to their re-election.

Varied regional interests

The sheer size of America and the diversity of its population makes it nearly impossible for a party hoping for nationwide appeal to expect its members to take the same positions on all issues or to have the same policy priorities. A Democrat seeking election from a constituency covering New York City would find it difficult to succeed if she adopted the same policy positions and priorities as a fellow Democrat in, say, rural Kansas. It would be folly for any party to expect candi-dates to do otherwise.

Primary elections

Unlike in the United Kingdom, parties in the United States do not have the power to choose who represents them in the elec-tions for Congress. This decision is taken by the voters in each state or district in *primary elections.* In the months preceding the main Congressional elections, candidates hoping to

become their party's official nominee, fight other party hopefuls in a primary election. The winner becomes the Democrat
or Republican candidate in the general election. In most cases
only voters registered as a Democrat or a Republican (on reg-
istering to vote Americans can choose to register as a
Democrat, a Republican or an Independent) can cast a ballot
in the party's primary. These are known as *closed* primaries.
Some areas still hold *open* primaries, where voters may
choose which primary they participate in, regardless of their
registered affiliation.

At the start of the twentieth century, primary elections
were far from standard across the United States. However, as
the years passed, an increasing number of state-level party
offices adopted primary elections to choose their candidates.
This strengthened the tendency towards candidate-centred
campaigns in the subsequent general election; many of the
decisions candidates make about their campaign (main policy
positions, sources of funding, the staff hired and campaign
structures) need to be made early on in the primary campaign.
During the primary election, as a candidate's opponents are
from the same party, the aim of the campaign is to distinguish
the candidate from her challengers, to show why, in ideology
or character, she would make a better representative or
senator than the other members of her own party. The focus
is on the candidate rather than the party. Once the primary
election is won, while candidates can change their strategy
between the primary and general election, whether to shore
up their party's core support or to lure voters away from their
opponent, much of their campaign remains based on their
own attributes rather than those of their party.

Who wins?

There are over 500,000 elected officials in the United States, only 542 of which serve at the federal level: the President and Vice-President of the United States, 100 Senators, 435 Representatives and 5 delegates from the US territories (Puerto Rico, American Samoa, US Virgin Islands and Guam) and Washington DC (delegates can sit in the House of Representatives but are not allowed to vote). Consequently, with so few positions of influence available, competition for election to Congress is intense. Any citizen of the United States who has reached the allotted age (25 for House elections and 30 for the Senate) can stand for election. A candidate wishing to be the nominee of one of the major parties must first win the appropriate primary election or other chosen system of selection in the case of a minor party. Anyone gathering the appropriate number of signatures as established by state law can stand as an independent in the general election. The only further restriction is that a candidate must be a resident of the state they are hoping to represent.

So how does a US citizen improve their chances of being elected to Congress?

Be the Democrat or Republican nominee

While parties in the United States are less dominant than their counterparts in Western Europe, they still play a fundamental role in American Government. In the modern era nearly all candidates elected to Congress have been the nominee of either the Democrat or Republican Party. Since 1955, only five candidates have been elected to the House or Senate without the nomination of one of the two main parties. There are several reasons for this phenomenon.

The first reason for the consistent election of one of the two main party candidates is that the parties can provide nominees with the resources and organisation necessary to run an effective campaign. State-level party offices have ready a network of volunteers and contacts to support the party's nominee and they can supply a limited amount of campaign funds. Most crucially, the candidate can run under the banner of the official Republican or Democrat Party. Except where there is a notable independent candidate, the two major party nominees will receive far more media coverage than any third party campaign. In many ways this is a self-perpetuating trend; the media, wanting to focus on campaigns of the serious contenders will turn to the major party candidates, not because they are better people or more able campaigners than any independent, but because the candidate with a major party label is usually the winner. This perception is relayed to the public via increased media coverage. The majority of voters, not wishing to waste their vote on a no-hoper will be drawn to the Democrat or Republican candidate. The perception that major party candidates are the only viable ones is reinforced by the resources parties can supply candidates with.

Even with a rise in the number of voters considering themselves politically independent, the majority of Americans still view themselves, to varying degrees, Democrat or Republican. Table 2.2 shows the changes in party identification among the electorate (1952–98). While candidates cannot assume that a voter identifying with their party will automatically vote for them in the election, it is clear that as long as voters perceive electoral politics essentially as a choice between Democrats and Republicans, those parties' candidates will have an enormous advantage over most independents at election time.

Table 2.2 Party identification 3-point scale 1952–98. Generally speaking, do you usually think of yourself as a Republican, a Democrat, an Independent, or what?

Year	'52	'54	'56	'58	'60	'62	'64	'66	'68	'70	'72	'74	'76	'78	'80	'82	'84	'86	'88	'90	'92	'94	'96	'98
Democrat (%)	57	56	50	56	52	54	61	55	55	54	52	52	52	54	52	55	48	51	47	52	50	47	52	51
Independent (%)	6	7	9	7	10	8	8	12	11	13	13	15	15	14	13	11	11	12	11	10	12	11	9	11
Republican (%)	34	33	37	33	36	35	30	32	33	32	34	31	33	30	33	32	39	36	41	36	38	41	38	37
Apolitical (%)	3	4	4	4	2	4	1	1	1	1	1	3	1	3	2	2	2	2	2	2	1	1	1	2

Source: The National Election Studies.

Be the incumbent

One of the most striking features of modern Congressional elections is the high number of members of Congress who gain re-election. This is particularly true in the House where the re-election rates frequently exceeded 90 per cent. The factors which explain this trend are known as *incumbency advantages*.

The first advantage which incumbents have over their challengers in both primary and general elections is that, in the majority of cases, they will be better known than their opponents. While in office incumbents have either two or six years worth of television appearances, public meetings and publicity to get their name and, hopefully, their achievements known. Their opponents will have only months or even weeks to try to gain name recognition.

Incumbents are aided further in the promotion of their name and image by the resources which come with the job. Members of Congress have a sizeable staff in both Washington DC and their home-state offices. While challengers will have to find money for items such as stationary and postage costs, the Government provides this for members of Congress. The *franking privilege* (the ability to send mail to constituents free of charge) designed to allow members of Congress to keep their constituents informed of the actions of their representatives, has often caused controversy. The law states that the franking privilege cannot be used for the purpose of electioneering or sending any mail which 'specifically solicits political support for the sender or any other person or any political party, or a vote or financial assistance for any candidate for any public office'.[1] However, as critics point out, the difference between a letter informing constituents of what their representative has been doing on their behalf and one 'soliciting political support' can be fine indeed. It is noticeable that those incumbents facing the closest election battles are often the ones who use the privilege most.[2]

Incumbents have a number of other institutional advantages over their opponents, including government-subsidised travel between the constituency and the Capitol and radio and television facilities in Congress which allow members to appear on local media while in Washington. However, perhaps the greatest advantage incumbents possess is that they can actually do the job. Representatives have two and Senators have six years during which to impress their constituents. As will be discussed in chapter 3, members try to pass legislation or take policy positions in speeches which will win the favour of their constituents and they attempt to ensure that any programme distributing grants or other benefits includes their own state or district (and their role in obtaining benefits well publicised). Even more important is the part of the job known as *constituency service*, which entails responding to the queries, complaints or problems of individual constituents. Addressing the concerns of individual voters may seem a fruitless task in a nation as large as the United States, but as former House Speaker Tip O'Neil explained

> A politician learns that if a constituent calls about a problem, even if it's a streetlight out, you don't tell them to call City Hall. You call City Hall. Members of the House learn this quicker than anyone else because they only have a two-year term. They learn that if you don't pay attention to the voters, you soon will find yourself right back there with them.[3]

The decline of party identification in the modern era has made such personal advantages even more important. With Republican and Democrat nominees unable to rely solely on their party label, the ability to herald their own achievements while in office gives any incumbent a head start over their often less experienced challengers.

Spend more money than your opponents

Running for national office in the United States is an expensive business. In the 2000 Congressional election over $694 million was spent by the major party candidates, an increase of 42 per cent from 1998.[4] The average expenditure of candidates for the House of Representatives was $474,019 with their Senate counterparts spending, on average, $4,787,863. In the race for the Senate in New Jersey, Democrat Jon Corzine spent over $54 million on his campaign alone, compared to the $4 million spent by his opponent. Corzine was elected by a margin of 3 per cent.

The cost of running for office can be partly explained by the sheer size of the United States. While candidates for the House of Representatives have on average 500,000 voters to reach, Senate hopefuls often face a potential electorate running into millions. In the 2000 election, candidates running for the Senate in California had a formidable 24 million citizens who were eligible to vote. These potential voters need to be reached by the candidates either in person at rallies and meetings, over the telephone, by mail or through the media of television, radio and newspapers.

While the amount of money a candidate can spend is important in Congressional elections, it is not enough on its own. In the 2000 campaign, Rick Lazio spent over $33 million, some $7 million more than his opponent Hillary Clinton, in the race for the vacant Senate seat for New York. Lazio lost by 12 per cent of the vote. Despite his monetary advantage, Hillary Clinton's high personal profile, mistakes by the Lazio campaign and the Democrat vote holding strong, led to Clinton's victory.

Despite such instances, the link between spending power and success is undeniable. In 2000, winning candidates for the House spent, on average, $653,183 compared to $267,145 for losing major party candidates. In the race for the Senate the figures were $6,405,755 and $3,119,413, respectively. The differences become even more stark when the closest of races are examined. In races where the winner was elected with 55 per cent of the vote or less, winners spent, on average, 64 per cent more than their nearest competitors.

Matters are further complicated when the amount of money raised and spent by incumbents is examined. In the 2000 House elections incumbents spent nearly three times more, on average, than their challengers; Senate incumbents spent around twice as much as their challengers. In the twenty-nine races where sitting Senators contested their seats, only three were outspent by their challengers. This trend of incumbents achieving a monetary advantage over their opponents can lead us to one of two conclusions: If incumbents are achieving high re-election rates largely due to their institutional advantages (discussed above) and *also* spend, on average, more money than their challengers, this would suggest a link between the amount of money spent and success in the election, which might not be the complete picture. Alternatively, the spending figures may suggest that one of the reasons incumbents are so successful in gaining re-election is that they can raise and spend more money than their challenger. The reality is probably a combination of both.

Incumbents are able to achieve this spending advantage due to their ability to raise more funds than their opponents. In 2000 House incumbents out-raised their challengers by four to one, with their Senate equivalents having a two-to-one advantage. Money for election campaigns usually come from one or more of three sources: the candidate's own pocket,

---

Box 2.1   Jon Corzine v. Bob Franks, New Jersey Senate 2000

The 2000 race for the vacant Senate seat in New Jersey was notable for one reason – the record amount of money spent by the eventual winner, Democrat Jon Corzine. The vast majority of Corzine's funds came not from the usual source of Political Action Committees and individual donations but from the multi-millionaire candidate himself.

Corzine spending during the general election campaign totalled in excess of $60 million, $3 million of which was spent on election day alone in an attempt to make sure that Democrat voters went to the polls. A former chairman of investment bank Goldman Sachs and Co., Corzine had amassed his vast fortune on Wall Street. In contrast, the Republican candidate Congressman Bob Franks managed to raise and spend less than a tenth of his opponent's total.

During the campaign, in a state where over half of voters are registered as independents (the rest being equally divided between Democrats and Republicans), Corzine used his fortune to bombard voters with messages advocating increased government support of education and healthcare. His opponent instead focused on the need to root out 'wasteful Washington spending'.

Inevitably attention focused on the money being spent by Corzine. The candidate claimed that his largely self-funded campaign meant that, once elected, he would be indebted to no-one except the voters themselves. The Republicans pointed to the fact that over half of Corzine's $800 million wealth was tied up in Goldman Sachs stock, and consequently his former company would 'call his every move'. Corzine promised to liquidate his stock if elected.

Despite the massive imbalance of spending in the campaign, the race was a close one. Corzine won, but only by 51 per cent to 48 per cent of the vote.

donations by members of the public and contributions from outside groups such as businesses, trade unions and pressure groups. It is the last of these which has caused the most controversy in recent years.

Interest group or business donations are regulated under campaign law dating from the Federal Election Campaign Act of 1971 (amended in 1974 and 1976). Any group wishing to donate money to candidates for federal office must first form a Political Action Committee (PAC) which must be registered with the Federal Election Commission (FEC), the body charged with supervising elections. PACs are limited in how much money they can donate to any one candidate; currently they can give up to $5,000 to a single candidate per election (individuals are restricted to donations of $1,000 under the same law). The aim of the regulation was to ensure that rich groups, particularly corporations could not attempt to buy undue influence over elected officials. How far this aim has been achieved will be examined in chapter 8.

Groups donate money to Congressional candidates for two main reasons: to aid the election of candidates sympathetic to their cause (or to aid the defeat of those whose policies they oppose) or to increase the likelihood of having influence over the member of Congress once in office. Both these goals give incumbents a number of advantages when raising funds. The first advantage is that incumbents are in office and can currently influence the workings of Congress, making them a more attractive prospect for a group or company hoping to influence the legislative process through political donations. The second advantage is that incumbents are statistically more likely to gain re-election. Apart from the most principled of groups, PACs are likely to find candidates with a good chance of winning more attractive prospects than a sympathetic outsider.

In the pursuit of influence, little will be gained from contributing to the funds of losing candidates. This attitude was reflected in the 2000 election when House incumbents, on average, received more than eight times the funds from PACs than did their challengers; for the Senate the advantage was six to one.

As the cost of running a successful campaign increased, the statutory limits on donations by PACs have proven to be only partially successful. Groups and wealthy individuals have managed to find four main ways to circumvent the law. Firstly, services which help the candidate more than would a simple $1,000 donation, can be offered free of charge. For example, catering for a fund-raising dinner, transport to move the candidate around the constituency, expensive direct mailing lists provided free of charge. Secondly, PACs engage in what is known as *bundling*. Rather than donate just the allowed $5,000, groups can instead collect the individual $1,000 donations of their members and, assuring the FEC that the money comes from individual members rather than the PAC's own funds, present a candidate with a collectively 'bundled' large gift of tens or hundreds of thousands of dollars. Thirdly, due to a Supreme Court ruling designed to protect freedom of speech, any group can spend as much money as they like either promoting or opposing a candidate, as long as there is no contact between the group and any of the candidates in order to co-ordinate their campaign. Finally, in order that the imposed limits do not prevent parties from encouraging a high turnout of voters on election day, the original 1970s law placed no limits on the amount of money which can be donated to local political parties to enable them to 'get out the vote'. Such donations are known as *soft money*.

Soft money has become a controversial issue in recent elections. The distinction between a party encouraging people to come out to vote and encouraging people to come out to vote *for their candidate* is a fine one. Consequently, donors have been quick to realise that one of the easiest ways to help a candidate is to make a large donation under the soft money law. The issue became a high profile one with Senator John McCain, who lost to George W. Bush in the 2000 Republican Presidential primary elections, placing it firmly on the national agenda. In 2001, McCain, along with Democrat Senator Russ Feingold, introduced legislation to bring soft money under the electoral regulations. After a long and sometimes bitter fight, Congress finally brought soft money under the law.[5]

Run a good campaign

Money is important for success; indeed without funds for the basics of a campaign victory is unlikely. However, as Rick Lazio discovered in New York, money cannot guarantee a seat in Congress. The characteristics of the local electorate, mood of the electorate nationally, the character and record of the candidates and the strength of their campaigns can all affect the eventual result.

Too often is party overlooked as a factor in elections to Congress. While it is true that the character and campaign of the individual candidate are important to success in elections in the United States, the party still has a large part to play. Republican candidates are regularly more successful than their Democrat challengers in the southern states and rural Midwest, while Democrats often receive in excess of 85 per cent of the African American vote and fare considerably better in urban rather than rural areas. There are still a few constituencies in which one of the two major parties fields candidates unopposed, so small is the chance of the opposing party winning the seat. Although part identification has declined in recent years, a vast majority of the population still identify themselves with one of the two major parties to some extent. Most candidates cannot rely solely on their party label for election (and it obviously has no effect in the primary campaign), but the predisposition of the electorate towards one party cannot be ignored in assessing election campaigns.

Coupled with the constituency electorate's party leanings is the effect of national politics on individual campaigns. The conventional wisdom agrees with Tip O'Neil when he states that 'all politics is local', and it is largely right, however national swings for or against one party can also have an effect. One such factor is the performance of the President. Traditionally, during presidential election years, observers believe that a party's performance in the Congressional elections will be affected by the performance of their candidate in the presidential elections. The Congressional party, benefit from the positive feeling towards their presidential candidate, and get pulled along on the successful President's coat-tails.

The performance of the winning presidential candidate's Congressional party in presidential election years is shown in Table 2.3a. Since 1948, while the winning Presidential candidate's party has often had success in that year's Congressional election, one is no guarantee of the other. Indeed in the last four elections the party which won the race for the White House has actually lost seats in the House of Representatives. One reason for this trend has been the growth of *split-ticket voting*, where voters vote for different parties for President and Congress in the same year.

Perhaps more notable are the results of the mid-term elections which take place between Presidential elections. As shown in Table 2.3b, the party which holds the White House

Table 2.3a   The coat-tails effect?

Year	Winning presidential candidate	Winning presidential candidate's party	Performance of winning presidential candidate's party (no. of seats)	
			House of Representatives	Senate
1948	Truman	Democrat	+75	+9
1952	Eisenhower	Republican	+22	+1
1956	Eisenhower	Republican	−2	No change
1960	Kennedy	Democrat	−21	No change
1964	Johnson	Democrat	+37	+1
1968	Nixon	Republican	+5	+6
1972	Nixon	Republican	+12	−2
1976	Carter	Democrat	+1	No change
1980	Reagan	Republican	+34	+12
1984	Reagan	Republican	+15	−1
1988	Bush (G.)	Republican	−2	No change
1992	Clinton	Democrat	−18	+1
1996	Clinton	Democrat	+9	−2
2000	Bush (G.W.)	Republican	−1	−4

tend to lose seats in Congress. Indeed, in all post-war mid-term elections, only once has the President's party not lost seats in the House. This often reflects a general dissatisfaction with the status quo which is usually taken out on the party which holds the White House.

Although national trends and the party leanings of the local electorate have a role to play, candidates for Congress would be unwise to rely purely on their party label to deliver victory in the general election. With the number of people strongly identifying with one of the major parties on the decline, the support of more and more 'floating voters' is there to be won by a good campaign.

Table 2.3b   Mid-term election performance of the President's party

Year	President	President's party	Performance of the President's party (no. of seats)	
			House of Representatives	Senate
1950	Truman	Democrat	−29	−6
1954	Eisenhower	Republican	−18	−1
1958	Eisenhower	Republican	−49	−13
1962	Kennedy	Democrat	−4	+3
1966	Johnson	Democrat	−47	−4
1970	Nixon	Republican	−12	+2
1974	Nixon	Republican	−48	−5
1978	Carter	Democrat	−15	−3
1982	Reagan	Republican	−26	+1
1986	Reagan	Republican	−5	−8
1990	Bush (G.)	Republican	−8	−1
1994	Clinton	Democrat	−52	−8
1998	Clinton	Democrat	+5	No change

By far the largest percentage of a candidate's expenditure goes on their media campaign. With a large electorate to reach with their message, newspapers, radio and television are an essential part of any serious modern Congressional campaign. Focus groups and opinion polls are frequently employed to ensure that the themes of advertising hit home with the public.

The theory in practice

On the surface, the election of 1994 seemed to upset much of the perceived wisdom of how Congressional elections are won and lost. One notable feature was the number of House incumbents who lost their seats in the election. Thirty-four incumbents (all Democrats) lost out to a Republican challenger in the general election, the highest figure since 1966. Four Democrats did not even make the general election, being defeated in the primary election before that. Many were replaced by candidates with limited or even no prior political experience. The most significant Democrat incumbent to fall in the general election was Tom Foley of Washington state. What made Foley's defeat stand out was that he was the Speaker of the House of Representatives, making him the biggest scalp the Republicans could claim.

Another feature of 1994 was the sheer size of swing towards the Republicans. The Democrats lost fifty-two seats in the House and eight in the Senate, the highest loss in either chamber since 1946. For the Democrats and President Clinton, 1994 represented an electoral disaster. While commentators had expected Republican gains, few had predicted the size of the landslide which occurred. The *frosh* class of 1995 (those elected to Congress for the first time in 1994) was unusually large; there were eighty-six in total, of whom seventy-three were Republican, and 90 per cent of those represented constituencies which had returned Democrats to the previous Congress.

The victorious Republicans claimed that the 1994 election defied the conventional wisdom that elections are won and lost on local issues. Republicans said that the election had been 'nationalised' by the *Contract with America*. By committing the whole House Republican Party to a specific collection of policies, the Republicans not only contrasted themselves from the 'do-nothing' Democrats, but gave the public a clear set of goals by which they could be judged and, ultimately, held accountable. The timing was particularly effective following the failure of President Clinton to pass his promised high profile healthcare reforms despite a Democrat majority in both chambers of Congress. Some of the newly elected Republicans saw the *Contract* as so central to their success that they wore laminated copies of the document around their necks and referred to it as their 'Bible'.

While there is no doubt that the 1994 elections handed the Republican Party a major victory, giving them complete control of Congress for the first time since the 1950s, and the number of Democrat seats which turned Republican was exceptionally large, we should not exaggerate the extent to which it defied previous electoral trends. Although a number of incumbents were defeated, the incumbent re-election rate still reached over 90 per cent in both House and Senate, a higher figure than in the previous election. While an incumbency success rate of 90 per cent is slightly down on the average figure for the 1980s, it is about average for the whole post-war period. Similarly, while the total number of Republican gains was high, it was not unprecedented in midterm elections; losses by one party in the House had reached forty-seven in 1958, 1966 and 1974 and the net gain of eight Senate seats for the Republicans had been equalled by the Democrats in 1986.

As far as the *Contract* is concerned, the evidence for its central importance to the subsequent electoral success is, at best, shaky. It is probable that the existence of the *Contract* helped the Republicans' overall image, but awareness of the document appears to be limited outside of the political community. In polls taken at the time, 71 per cent of those questioned had never even heard of the *Contract with America*, and of those who had, only 7 per cent said it was more likely to make them vote Republican, and 5 per cent claimed that it would actually deter them from supporting the party. Its effect is more likely to have been indirect, ensuring that Republicans across the nation campaigned on similar themes, aiding the prominence of these issues in the public's mind. There is evidence that the results of 1994 should be attributed more to the public voting *against* the Democrats and President Clinton rather than *for* the Republican agenda. One Republican Representative admitted that not realising this led to mistakes being made. 'When the Republicans held their very first conference after the election, there was a question I was dying to ask. And I've been kicking myself in the butt ever since for not asking it. I wanted to ask, "Did we win or did they lose?"'[6]

The subsequent elections of 1996, 1998 and 2000 followed most of the established electoral trends. Incumbency re-election rates remained around 90 per cent and there were no dramatic shifts in the party balance in either chamber. The Democrats did buck the trend by picking up seats at the 1998 mid-term elections, despite a Democrat incumbent in the White House. Overall, the traditional wisdom as to how campaigns are run, won and lost remains valid.

Summary

Elections to Congress are determined more by local issues and personality than any equivalent election in Western Europe. Such factors have been made even more central by the growth of primary elections to determine the nominees of the major parties. The ability to raise and spend significant amounts of money has also become an important determinant of electoral success. In addition, incumbents hold a large advantage over challengers, with re-election rates consistently reaching over 90 per cent. Despite this, the importance of the party should not be overlooked. The 1994 Congressional elections saw the Republicans take control of the House of Representatives and Senate for the first time since the 1952 election. Claims have been made that this success was due to the *Contract with America* which pledged Republican candidates to a national manifesto of policy pledges, although the evidence suggests that other factors were more important.

Notes

1 US Code, 39 USC Sec. 3210 (5C).
2 G. R. Simpson, 'Surprise! Top Frankers Also Have the Stiffest Challenges', *Roll Call* (22 October 1992) pp. 1, 15.
3 T. O'Neil, *All Politics is Local* (Holbrook MA: Bob Adams Inc., 1994) p. xvi.
4 Source: Common Cause (www.commoncause.org) and Federal Election Commission (www.fec.gov).
5 However, at the time of writing, there is still a chance that this law may be subject to a challenge in the courts.
6 Quoted in R. F. Fenno, *Learning to Govern: An Institutional View of the 104th Congress* (Washington DC: Brookings Institution Press, 1997), p. 30.

3

Representatives and Senators

Reader, suppose you were an idiot. And suppose you were a
member of Congress. But I repeat myself. (Mark Twain)

Once the November elections are over, the newly elected
Representatives and Senators gather the following January
for the start of the new Congress. Out of the thousands of
hopefuls who started the arduous process of campaigning in
the primary and general elections, only 535 people sit as
members of Congress for the next two years; 435 in the
House and 100 in the Senate. For most of those members, this
will not be a new experience; only one-third of the Senate's
seats are up for election at any one time (leaving two-thirds
of the Senate to continue their six-year term without the need
for re-election) and the majority of the other members of
Congress will be returning to their offices after successful re-
election. As discussed in the previous chapter, on average,
over 90 per cent of the Representatives and Senators who
choose to run for re-election are successfully returned to the
next Congress.

What sort of person gets elected?

To make an overgeneralisation, the typical person who wins election to Congress is a white male lawyer. It would appear, at first sight, that the second part of President Lincoln's famous proclamation at Gettysburgh of 'government of the people – by the people – for the people' has yet to be fulfilled. However, this is still a matter for debate. The 2000 elections ensured that the 107th Congress would contain an unprecedented number of women: 61 in the House of Representatives and 13 in the Senate. In addition, the 107th Congress benefited from 38 African American and 21 Hispanic members, all in the House. While this is an improvement on ten or twenty years ago, Congress is still some way from reflecting the wide and varied demographics of American society. While women, African Americans and Hispanics represent 51 per cent, 12 per cent and 12 per cent of the overall population respectively, they contribute 17 per cent, 9 per cent and 5 per cent of the members of the United States Congress.[1]

In terms of members' previous occupations, Congress is an institution dominated by lawyers and businessmen. In the 106th Congress (1999–2001), when asked to list their previous occupations, over 40 per cent of Senators and Representatives claimed to be lawyers. The next largest category, with 35 per cent, was business or banking, with politicians coming in third (Box 3.1).[2] Several reasons can be suggested for this dominance by the legal and business communities. People from these occupations often benefit from their connections in the worlds of politics and business which are vital for building support and collecting campaign funds. They will often have already acquired the public speaking, negotiating and networking skills needed in the political arena, and, perhaps most importantly, they are given an advantage in having careers and salaries which allow them to take the time off to dedicate to an election campaign. It also may be that lawyers and businessmen are looked to and trusted to fulfil the role of member of Congress, quite simply because they resemble the majority of those who are already doing the job; in other words, they act and appear in the way people have come to expect their representatives to behave.

Box 3.1   Previous occupations of members of the 106th Congress (members may list more than one)

- 217 lawyers
- 184 businessmen/bankers
- 124 public service/ politicians
- 99 educators
- 28 farmers/ranchers
- 24 estate agents
- 17 journalists
- 17 medical professionals
- 10 law enforcement officers
- 9 engineers
- 5 miscellaneous fields

- 3 professional athletes
- 3 skilled labor
- 3 healthcare providers
- 2 actors/entertainers
- 2 artists
- 2 clergy
- 2 military officers
- 1 aerospace professional
- 1 labour official
- 1 homemaker
- 1 secretary

Source: Congressional Quarterly Weekly Report

Should this difference between the diversity of the American population and the relative homogeneity of the members of Congress be a cause for concern? Critics argue that true representation cannot be achieved while the nation's legislature is dominated by people from one section of society. However well-intentioned any member of Congress tries to be, they will never fully understand the position of different groups or individuals because they have never been through their situations or experiences. It is argued that this is not just a matter of how each representative casts their vote, but one of which issues or problems are seen as important enough to have a prominent place on the national agenda. In short, with Congress, the business world and the mainstream media dominated by wealthy white men, politics will inevitably have a wealthy white male agenda.

Alternatively, it can be argued that representation in a democracy does not require the legislature to be a reflection of society. How a member of Congress behaves, casts their votes and which issues they choose to prioritise is far more important than their gender, colour or class. If a representative is not fulfilling these roles to the satisfaction of the majority of their constituents, they will not be re-elected. Indeed, the Senator for somewhere like California has the job of representing voters from all possible communities and groups. It is not possible for a member to physically resemble all the people they represent. It is also claimed that it is a mistake to assume that on any one issue there is a distinct male, female, African American or Hispanic view; people from all sections of society have differing opinions on all issues, a fact which would not be changed by a more diverse Congress. Business and law are both professions where you are likely find some of the most well-educated and talented Americans, it is argued that it is to Congress' credit that it attracts the brightest individuals when careers other than politics are likely to pay better. Finally, it is contended that Congress is becoming more and more diverse, with the percentages of women and minorities represented rising steadily. Furthermore, while many lawyers are elected, the 107th Congress (2001–2003) also included members with previous experience as, among others, a florist, a steelworker, a riverboat captain, a hotel bellhop, a taxicab driver and a race-track blacksmith.[3]

Members' goals

On election night, once the votes have been counted, each successful candidate will make a victory speech to their supporters and, through the media, to their wider constituency. Most of these speeches follow the same pattern, the candidate will thank the voters for their support and acknowledge the work of their staff and volunteers, they will thank and extend a hand of friendship to their opponent and his or her supporters, promising to represent all the people of the district or state. They will touch on the key issues of the campaign, promising to concentrate their efforts to make a difference in these particular areas and finally they will pledge themselves to working as hard as they can in the interests of all constituents. On election night, these promises are easy to make; achieving them once in Congress is another matter entirely.

Whatever is said on election night, is it possible to make judgements on the priorities and goals of members of Congress? For the majority of members, their main priority is to be re-elected in two or six years time. In his influential text *Congress: The Electoral Connection*, David Mayhew paints a picture of members of Congress as 'single-minded seekers of re-election'.[4] According to Mayhew, while in office, members engage in advertising, credit-claiming and position-taking in order to make a favourable impression on the voters back home; their decisions made with a constant eye on the reaction of their constituents. While he accepts that other motivations will exist in Congress, Mayhew argues that

the electoral goal has an attractive universality to it. It has to
be the *proximate* goal of everyone, the goal that must be
achieved over and over if other ends are to be entertained.
One former Congressman writes, 'All members of Congress
have a primary interest in getting re-elected. Some members
have no other interest'. Re-election underlies everything else,
as indeed it should if we are to expect that the relation
between politicians and public will be one of accountability.[5]

If this image of members of Congress dedicated solely to
retaining their jobs at the next election is true, should it worry
the American public? The quotation above suggests that it
should not; that in a democracy it is the job of members of
Congress to represent the wishes of their voters. The democratic principle of accountability means members would be
failing in their role if they did not keep a constant watch on
how their behaviour will be viewed by their constituents
and modify their actions accordingly. However, Mayhew's
study also raises some worrying questions about the role of
Congress as the nation's legislature. Can Congress with each
of its members dedicated to looking after their own fortunes
and those of their constituents be capable of making laws in
the interest of the nation as a whole? It has been argued that
activities such as advertising and position-taking, which may
play well with the folks back home, do little to help make good
laws. Particularly when legislation is complicated, one could
argue that it is the job of the member of Congress to use their
own judgement to lead, rather than follow, their constituents.

There is, however, much material to suggest that the image
of members of Congress as 'single-minded seekers of re-
election' is an oversimplification. Richard Fenno produced a
model where legislators have not one, but three primary
goals.[6] For Fenno, the goal of re-election is joined by two

others: making good policy and gaining influence within Congress. Naturally, if taking a position on a policy or casting a vote in a certain direction is likely to have a direct effect on their election chances, members will change their behaviour accordingly. However, there will also be many situations where a member's actions will not have such an impact, where an issue has no interest for the voters at home or where there is no guide as to what the opinion of constituents would be. At those times, members are freed from concerning themselves with re-election and can pursue their other goals of making good public policy and improving their own standing within Congress. There is one further question as to what extent members' behaviour is influenced by interest groups who supply much needed funds for election campaigns. This will be dealt with in chapter 8.

Achieving the goals

Whatever the specific priorities a member of Congress decides on, they face a number of barriers to achieving their goals. The main obstacle to reaching their ends is the fact they are only one of 100 legislators if in the Senate or one of 435 in the House. For any chosen policy to become law or money to be appropriated for projects, the approval of a majority of both the House of Representatives and Senate is required. Each member's pet projects or key priorities must compete with those of all the other members for their colleagues' support and for time on the Congressional schedule. During the election period, candidates across the country make promises of what they will achieve if elected, however there must be doubt as to exactly how much difference one person can make. This section discusses some of the ways in which legislators try and overcome these barriers and successfully achieve the goals of making good public policy and ensuring their eventual re-election.

Policy specialisation

When the fate of a bill is finally decided on the floor of the House or the Senate, all members are, in theory, equal. All have one vote and are free to cast it in any way they see fit, or not cast it at all if that is what they wish. However, in practice, there is much more to determining what becomes law than the final vote in either chamber. In these areas all members cannot be said to be equal. Hundreds of different policy areas are dealt with by every Congress, with members having the opportunity to debate and vote on issues as diverse as taxation, environmental policy, education, gun law and foreign affairs. It quickly becomes clear to new members that it will not be possible for them to have a significant influence (beyond the right to speak or cast their vote) in all areas of policy. This inevitably leads to members concentrating their efforts on a few carefully chosen issues, a process known as *policy specialisation.*

Each member of Congress faces many demands on their time and that of their staff. It is simply not possible for them to dedicate their time and resources to gaining expertise in every area of policy. While they will be expected to have an opinion and some knowledge on any given issue that is raised in an election campaign, if a member hopes to become fully active in the legislative process they will usually dedicate their time and resources to a few areas.

The choice of issues will largely be determined by the type of constituency a member of Congress represents. Here the goals of re-election and good public policy can coincide. For instance, a Representative whose constituency covers downtown urban New York would gain little benefit from specialising in agricultural policy, however interesting the issue may be. Alternatively, a Senator from a rural state whose primary occupation was farming would hardly be promoting their constituents' interests (or their own re-election chances) if at least one of their key issues was not related to agriculture.

The choice of which issues a member concentrates on may also be influenced by their backgrounds and interests. They may choose to dedicate time to policies in which they have prior experience or expertise, or to issues which they personally feel are important. Especially in the Senate, the choice of speciality can also be influenced by their colleagues choices. There is evidence to show that Senators will try to specialise in different areas to those chosen by the other Senator from their state, so to make sure they have their own territory marked out for the media and voters to see.[7]

At the heart of policy specialisation by members is the committee system of House and Senate, which will be considered in detail in the next chapter. The committees are the engine room of Congress where legislation is researched and formulated. To a large extent the committees are the bodies who decide which legislation will be put to a vote of the House or Senate and which will quietly die. Consequently, for most members, if they are to have any significant influence over an area of policy they must ensure they have a seat on the relevant committee, as it is here that many of the key decisions are made. When first elected to Congress members will supply their party leadership with a wish-list of committees on which they would like to serve. The party leaders will then allocate committee places, with the level of demand for each seat determining how far they can accommodate each legislator's request.

The allocation of committee seats will go a long way in narrowing the areas in which a member can effectively specialise. While there is nothing to stop a member becoming knowledgeable and speaking out on an issue not under their committees' jurisdiction, the direct influence they can exercise is likely to be limited. Instead, if used to its potential, the committee system will help policy specialisation by giving legislators an arena in which they can both accumulate knowledge and influence policy. Members' influence over their key issue area will rise as they gain a reputation for being an expert in the field and move up the committee hierarchy. When this influence is in a policy area of importance to their constituents, it will also have the effect of aiding their re-election.

Constituency service

The choice of policy areas to focus on can be viewed as one way of serving constituents and aiding re-election, as can voting in accord with the wishes of the folks back home. There are also ways in which members of Congress can help their constituency more directly.

The most basic of these is constituency *case work*. Case work entails dealing with the problems or requests of individual constituents. Members receive thousands of letters, emails and telephone calls from their voters every year. Many of these will be communications expressing an opinion on an issue of importance to them or voicing approval or displeasure over the actions of their representative on Capitol Hill. Others will be requesting help for a wide variety of reasons; there may be complaints that a social security or pension cheque has not arrived, a constituent may be having problems with some level of government or a student may request information for a project they are researching. Any member of

Congress with the intention of being re-elected will ensure that their staff do their utmost to help with each and every problem, even if it is not something which is directly under their control. The gratitude a member will receive from that voter, if their office is seen to be interested or even go out of its way to help, will be greater than any credit which would be received by casting a particular vote or making a rousing speech. Alternatively, if the member's office is seen to be unhelpful or not interested in an individual's problems, the negative effect can outweigh years of good work. The assumption is that a pleased constituent will tell their family and friends about the episode helping to create an image of their member of Congress as someone who cares. A disgruntled voter who feels ignored will also make sure their neighbours know.

Members will also be pro-active in making sure they create an image of a legislator serving their constituency. Regular visits home, appearances at local public, social or sporting events and a high media presence all promote the member as a good 'local' Senator or Representative. Every member maintains at least one office in their constituency (often more than one for Senators from a large state) to allow easy contact with the voters. Building up a good local reputation can create a strong personal following for the member which can ensure re-election. Over the years it has been noticeable that, when polled, voters consistently express a much higher opinion of their own Senators and Representatives than they do of Congress as a whole. This can be partly attributed to the amount of effort members put into serving, or appearing to serve, their constituents.

Pork barrel

The most controversial of ways in which members serve their constituents, but perhaps the most effective in terms of building a positive image, is what is know as *pork barrel*. Pork barrel (so called because the first recorded instance actually involved barrels of pork) is a term used for federally funded projects which a Senator or Representative acquires for their constituency to help with their re-election. These can include projects such as the building of a new hospital, the construction of a new highway bringing jobs and investment, money to help with cleaning a dirty river or assistance to local businesses. Members can be particularly successful at bringing home such benefits to their constituency if they have a place on any committee in charge of distributing such projects or funds.

Critics of Congress argue that much of this spending is wasteful as it directs taxpayers' money to districts with members on the right committee rather than to places which genuinely need such investment. The term 'pork barrel' is, however, a subjective one. What to one person may seem the much needed investment of federal funds into a suitable project in a needy part of the country, to their opponents will be politically motivated pork barrel. Whatever the incentive, members will frequently attempt to claim credit back home for some project or funding their district or state benefited from which is partly due to their intervention. There is no better photo opportunity for a member of Congress than the opening of a new highway, dam, hospital or community project supported by federal funds.

This issue of pork barrel lies at the heart of the debate surrounding the duties and goals of a member of Congress. All 435 House members and 100 Senators play two, often conflicting, roles. They are members of the federal legislature which is given the sole responsibility for making national laws by the Constitution, but they are also representatives of specific local areas whether that be a district or state. When federally funded programmes or initiatives are distributed will members be fulfilling their role properly if they fight to benefit the constituents whom they represent or by seeking to serve the national good, even if that means their own voters will not gain? The issue is further muddied by the fact that what constitutes the greatest need is often a matter for debate and interpretation, especially when demand for federal help outstrips the available funds.

Gaining influence within the chamber

Aside from any personal gratification that may be achieved, the goal of gaining influence within the chamber is largely a means to an end. While being awarded a seat on a committee and becoming active in its deliberations concerning specific policy areas is an important part of a member being able to shape the policies passed by Congress, it is only a first step. Any proposal a member wishes to make may face opposition from other members on the committee or from outside, it will also face stiff competition for a prominent place on both the committee's agenda and the Congressional agenda as a whole. Thousands of proposals are made every Congress by members looking to promote their own or their constituents' interests, but with only two years (the length of a Congress) to complete the journey from bill to law, the majority will fall by the wayside, never making it to a final vote in the House or Senate.

Any member entering Congress for the first time will find there is stiff competition to get their voice heard on any one issue and their priorities considered ahead of the many others on the agenda. This is especially true in the House where a legislator is only one voice in a chamber of 435 members. The first job of any member hoping to exert influence within their chamber is to learn the procedures of Congress. It is virtually impossible for a frosh (the term for a first-term legislator) member to personally convince every other legislator necessary to get their bill or proposal considered and then successfully passed through Congress. What they can do is learn the intricacies of the legislative process and which key positions or people hold the most power over such matters as scheduling or are in a position to persuade others. By developing their knowledge of Congress and their relationships with other members, frosh legislators can improve their chances of achieving their goals.

Once members have a few years of service behind them they can start to move into positions of authority either within their committees or party themselves. These topics will be dealt with in more detail in chapters 4 and 5. Suffice to say that posts such as subcommittee or committee chair, or a position of authority within one of the parties bring with them an increased influence over the content and scheduling of legislation. Under the process of *seniority* members move up the roster of their committees and subcommittees the longer they serve, until reaching the chair or, in the case of the members not belonging to the majority party, the ranking minority position.

Without achieving a formal position of power within Congress, members can begin to assert influence by gaining a reputation of expertise in their chosen areas of policy; many issues are complex and no legislator can hope to become an expert in all fields. When casting a vote for a particular piece of legislation, non-expert members wish to be assured that the law they are voting for is a good one, that their vote will not be tied to an unforeseen negative outcome by future opponents. By gaining a reputation of a knowledgeable and trustworthy legislator on a particular issue, a member can potentially increase their influence over the decisions of their colleagues.

Staff support

To aid their efforts to represent constituents, make good public policy or make their way within Congress, all members are given a great deal of support. Along with the franking privilege and funds to visit their constituency on a regular basis, all members and both parties are given good staff support. Each member establishes their own office and hires the staff to fill it. The budget they are given is set according to the size of their constituency. How much is spent on the Washington office and how much on its constituency equivalent is entirely up to the individual. Currently, there are approximately 24,000 Congressional staff workers serving members, committees and the party leaderships, an increase of some 18,000 since 1960.[8] The average House member employs 14 staff, the Senate average is 34.

In addition to personal, committee and party staff, members are supported by a number of legislative agencies. The Congressional Research Service (CRS), the Congressional Budget Office (CBO) and the General Accounting Office (GAO) are all non-partisan offices who will give support to any member looking to research Congressional activity or to write a bill. They are especially helpful in providing expert or technical advice on policy detail or helping staff to frame legislation in the correct legal language.

Reconciling conflicting goals

While the theory of the aims and objectives of members of Congress may seem straightforward, the decision-making process for individuals can be a delicate matter of judgement. A member's constituents which can number, for Senators, in the millions, will rarely be of one mind when it comes to how their elected officials should act. Members must make judgements about their constituents' preferences when it comes to expressing opinions, casting votes or choosing which issues to concentrate on. Subjects such as abortion or gun control often split voters evenly but raise strong feelings. When members decide that an issue is of little importance to their constituency and thus leave them free to act according to their conscience, how can they be sure that two years down the line events have not transpired to place the subject at the centre of an opponent's election campaign? Members of Congress must make considered judgements on a wide range of topics. Two examples can help illustrate some of the subtleties involved in Congressional decision making.

The impeachment of President Clinton

Following allegations of impropriety by President Clinton concerning the so-called 'Whitewater' land deals he, his wife and business partners had made in his home state of Arkansas, an independent council was established to look into the President's behaviour. Failing to find any evidence against the President over Whitewater, the council, Kenneth Starr, began to widen the scope of his investigation. What he discovered was that during a sexual harassment case brought early in his Presidency, Bill Clinton had denied suggestions that he had an affair with White House intern Monica

Lewinsky. The case actually had little to do with the intern and the denial raised little publicity until Starr revealed that he had evidence that Lewinsky had indeed been involved with the President, a fact which suggested that the President had lied before a Grand Jury. The independent council submitted his report to the House of Representatives in September 1998 accusing the President of obstructing justice.

The US Constitution gives Congress the power to remove the President from office in the event he is proven to have committed 'high crimes and misdemeanours'. First the House of Representatives must impeach the President by majority vote, the Senate will then hold a trial and, if found guilty by a two-thirds majority, the President is removed from office. Following the allegations in Starr's report, the House held hearings, deliberated and finally voted to impeach President Clinton. The Senate began its trial, but, with public opinion swinging firmly behind the President, it failed to achieve even a majority in the vote to remove him from office.

In opinion polls, the public far from approved of the President's action, but a large majority felt that his actions fell well short of the 'high crimes and misdemeanours' needed to impeach. The most common feeling was that this was a man who had seriously erred in his private life, but was still doing a good job as President. Indeed, although nearly 60 per cent of the public believed that the President had lied about his affair with Lewinsky, his job approval ratings rose dramatically during the crisis from 48 per cent before the allegations of infidelity to a high of 70 per cent in February 1999, at the height of the action against him. They were never to fall below 50 per cent again. In polls, 68 per cent felt that Congress should make the debate over social security its main priority with only 23 per cent thinking impeachment as or more important. Consistently 60 per cent of the public felt Congress should not remove him from office and, tellingly, 64 per cent believed that most members of Congress had lied to someone about having an extramarital affair.[9]

If members of Congress are so wedded to the views of their constituents when deciding how to act, why did a majority of the House of Representatives defy public opinion and vote to impeach President Clinton? Were they not worried that taking such a position would hurt their standing in the eyes of the voters? As with many actions taken by Congress, there is no simple answer. Many claimed a strong personal feeling that the President had betrayed his office by perjuring himself and lying to the nation. It was, they argued, their duty as a member of Congress to uphold the Constitution and proceed against the President. However, the actual vote on impeachment turned out to be more about party ties than personal conscience. The House divided on the issue largely on party lines with all but five Republicans voting to impeach and all but five Democrats voting to acquit. Party allegiances and Washington politics took precedence over public opinion for three reasons.

Firstly, it seemed unlikely that one member's vote on the issue would have little importance in the 2000 Congressional elections where local issues tend to take centre stage. Except for staunch supporters or opponents of Bill Clinton, would people really change their vote in the Congressional elections over the impeachment of the President? It seemed unlikely and certainly no one should lose their seat over it. Indeed the most likely arena for the decision to have any salience would be the primary elections, where voting with the majority of fellow party members could not be seen as detrimental, although voting against the party could. Secondly, House members were in a no-lose situation, if they voted to impeach it would still be the Senate who had to decide whether the President would be removed from office or not. The House action was always one step removed from the final decision on Clinton's fate. Finally, for many Republicans, the opinion polls could not be totally believed; surely, they argued, support could not keep holding up for a President who in their eyes has not only acted immorally, but had perjured himself and lied to the American people. In any event, plunging the Clinton Presidency into further crisis shortly before the end of his term in office would do little harm to the Republican candidates for the presidency and Congress in the year 2000.

By the time the Senate trial came to a close it was clear that the early public support of the President was no freak and, accordingly, the vote went against removing him from office. What opponents of Clinton had trumpeted as a case of perjury and obstruction of justice which threatened the dignity of the White House, the public had clearly seen as a political sex scandal of more tabloid proportions. What the episode can show us is that to perceive of Congressional behaviour as a direct reflection of what constituents want was, in this particular instance, only part of the picture.

Term limits

For anyone contending the primary objective of any member of Congress is to be consistent re-election at all costs, it may be surprising to find that the Republican Party's 1994 *Contract with America* contained a commitment to introduce term limits. Under the proposals, after serving two consecutive terms in the Senate or either three or six (members were to be given two options to debate) consecutive terms in the House, members would be barred from running for re-election. The idea behind the scheme was to counter the ability of incumbents to be elected time and time again due to the advantages of office, and to replace the long-term professional politician with fresh faces. Currently, eighteen states have similar restrictions on their own legislatures.

When the legislation came to a vote on the House floor, a majority of members voted for the proposal (227:224), but in this instance it was not enough for it to pass. The Supreme Court had ruled earlier in that year that Congressional term limits would require a Constitutional amendment rather than a simple law. According to the Constitution, amendments can only be adopted after gaining a two-thirds majority in both the House of Representatives and the Senate and the approval of two-thirds of the states. In this instance the proposed Constitutional amendment introducing Congressional term limits fell at the first hurdle, failing to achieve the required majority in the House. Forty Republicans joined the majority of Democrats to vote against, with 38 Democrats voting with the majority of Republicans in favour.

To say that the failure of the amendment was a foregone conclusion – that Representatives were not about to vote themselves out of job, even if it was in twelve-years time – misses the point that a majority of members appeared to be willing to do just that. We can only speculate as to their true motives. Many may have genuinely believed in the proposals as best for the nation, others, who planned to retire or move on within the next twelve years may have felt freed from protecting their own interests to vote in line with their own beliefs, those of their constituents or with their party leadership. There is also the distinct possibility that, as it became clear that the proposal stood no chance of gaining the two-thirds majority needed for it to progress, members were free to be seen supporting the idea, all along knowing that their jobs were safe from the consequences of it succeeding.

Of particular interest are those members who during the election campaign, as a matter of principle, pledged to impose their own term limits on themselves if the amendment was not successful. Some of them advocated a much shorter time limit than twelve years and so the strength of their commitment can already be seen. The results were mixed. For instance, Democrat Representative from Massachusetts Martin Meehan, first elected in 1992, pledged to stand down after eight years of service and George Nethercutt from Washington state, a Republican first elected in 1994, promised he would retire after only six years. Once ensconced in Congress both changed their minds and were still in office at the start of the 107th Congress in 2001. Nethercutt explained that 'experience . . . taught me that six years may be too short a time to do the job the people . . . elected me to do', Meehan argued that campaign finance reform was of such importance that he needed to stay in the House. In contrast to Nethercutt and Meehan, some House members did indeed stick to their own personal term limits. Elizabeth Furse of Oregon (elected in 1992) and Jack Metcalf of Washington state (elected in 1994) both declined to run for re-election after serving three consecutive terms.

What both of these examples illustrate is that, while we can legitimately make assumptions as to the goals and motives of members of Congress, it should not blind us from the fact that every situation is complex and different from next, and the way that each individual will respond to and judge the situation will also vary.

Summary

While Congress is becoming a more diverse body, the typical member is still a white male lawyer. Whether this is bad for American democracy is a matter for debate. Whatever the profile of the member, they are likely to have similar goals: to be re-elected, to make good policy and to gain influence within Congress. Which of these goals will be the priority will vary from issue to issue and will be a delicate matter for each member's judgement. Attention to the needs of constituents will always be important. To achieve any of these goals, members will need to specialise in certain areas of policy in order to get their voice heard and their proposals passed. At the heart of this is the committee system.

Notes

1 Population figures from the 2000 Census, Office of the Census, Washington DC (www.census.gov).

2 *Congressional Quarterly Weekly Report.*

3 Congressional Research Service, *Membership of the 107th Congress: A Profile*, order code: RS20760, p. 3.

4 D. R. Mayhew, *Congress: The Electoral Connection* (New Haven: Yale University Press, 1974).

5 Ibid, pp. 16–17.

6 R. F. Fenno Jr. *Congressmen in Committees* (Boston: Little, Brown, 1973).

7 W. Schiller, *Partners and Rivals* (Princeton: Princeton University Press, 2000).

8 See N. Ornstein, T. Mann and M. Malbin (eds.), *Vital Statistics on Congress, 1999–2000* (Washington DC: American Enterprise Institute, 1999).

9 Figure from Rasmussen Research; supplied at www.portraitofamerica. com.

4

The committee system

Congress in session is Congress on public exhibition, whilst Congress in its committee-rooms is Congress at work. (Woodrow Wilson)

Writing while still a postgraduate student, President Woodrow Wilson commented, 'Congressional government is committee government'. Committees are the engine rooms of Congress. In order to become law, every piece of legislation must ultimately face a vote in the chambers of House and Senate, but it is in the committee rooms that nearly all proposals take shape and where most proposals die. This chapter examines the role and the power of the committee, the legislators who populate these bodies and discusses whether the committee system as a whole is good for democracy in modern America.

Committee structure

There is no mention of committees in the Constitution, but it quickly became clear that if Congress was to function properly as the federal legislature, some sort of division of labour was going to be necessary. To overcome the problems inherent in getting a large group of legislators to deal effectively with a large range of detailed issues, the early stages of the legislative process are now delegated to committees.

It is the responsibility of the House of Representatives and Senate as a whole to determine the number and size of their own committees, although these decisions are now mainly made by the party leaderships before being ratified by the whole chamber. The number of Democrats and Republicans on each committee is worked out between the two leaderships, the figures broadly reflecting the balance between the two parties in the chamber as a whole. It is up to the individual parties to decide which of its members sits on which committee.

There are essentially five types of committees in Congress. *Standing committees* carry out the day-to-day work of reviewing the bills introduced into Congress, gathering information and framing the legislation to be put to the floor. These are the workhouses of Congress and will be examined in detail shortly. *Ad hoc committees* are other sources of legislation, these temporary bodies can be established to write and report legislation on specific topics. Once completing their task or running for a specified time, the ad hoc committee will then cease to exist. Such bodies are only used occasionally. *Select* or *special committees* are another type of temporary panel designed to look at a specific topic. Unlike ad hoc committees, select committees usually do not have the power to report legislation (although the Select Intelligence Committees of House and Senate have been made permanent and granted that power); instead they are mainly used to research a specific issue or to investigate the behaviour of the executive branch. One of the most noticeable select committees in recent years was the Senate Select Committee on

Presidential Campaign Activities, established in 1973 to investigate allegations made against President Nixon following the Watergate affair.

Like select committees, *joint committees* have no power to write legislation. They are investigating committees composed of members from both House and Senate. The only other committee which comprises both Senators and Representatives are the *conference committees*. Conference committees are temporary bodies, established to iron out the differences between the two chambers when both have passed slightly different versions of the same bill. We will look at these particular bodies in chapter 6.

Standing committees

In the 107th Congress there were nineteen standing committees and one permanent select committee in the House and sixteen in the Senate, each with its own area of policy to consider. These are set out in Box 4.1. At the start of the Congress each chamber determines the committees which will serve them over the next two years. Nearly every bill which is entered into either House or Senate will begin its journey in the committee concerned with that particular area of policy. For the majority of bills however, the committee will also mark the end of its journey. Committees act as the *gatekeepers* of Congress, deciding which legislation will be reported for consideration by the full chamber and which will die quietly with no further action.

On average, while 4,000 bills are entered into each Congress by its members, only about 400 complete the journey into law. The vast majority of these end their life at the committee stage. This is partly a political role, with the

Box 4.1 Congressional committees

Senate

House of Representatives

Standing Committees

Senate	House of Representatives
Agriculture, Nutrition and Forestry	Agriculture
Appropriations	Appropriations
Armed Services	Armed Services
Banking, Housing and Urban Affairs	Budget
Budget	Education and the Workforce
Commerce, Science and Transportation	Energy and Commerce
Energy and Natural Resources	Financial Services
Environment and Public Works	Government Reform
Finance	House Administration
Foreign Relations	International Relations
Governmental Affairs	Judiciary
Judiciary	Resources
Health, Education, Labor and Pensions	Rules
Rules and Administration	Science
Small Business	Small Business
Veterans' Affairs	Standards of Official Conduct
	Transportation and Infrastructure
	Veterans' Affairs
	Ways and Means

Special, select, and other Committees

Senate	House of Representatives
Indian Affairs Committee	Permanent Select Committee on Intelligence
Senate Select Ethics	Select Committee on Homeland Security
Senate Select Intelligence	
Senate Special Aging	

Joint Committees of Congress
Joint Economic Committee
Joint Printing Committee
Joint Taxation Committee

committee choosing the topics it wishes to see action on, and partly a matter of practicality; there is simply not the time to consider all areas of policy effectively during the life of a Congress. The issues chosen by the committee to take action on are determined by a number of factors. The personal preferences of committee members can be influential, allowing those with a seat on a relevant panel to help frame legislation they see as important. Pressure can mount on a committee to address a particular problem or issue from within Congress and also from outside sources such as the media, interest groups, the public or another branch of government. Alternatively, from its own investigations, the committee may identify areas where existing laws are not functioning properly and use their position in the legislative process to develop the suitable remedy.

Aside from the gate-keeping function, the primary purpose of committees is to research and write the legislation to be debated by the full chamber. The process by which this happens and its consequences is the topic of the following section.

The committees at work

Subcommittees

Even with the work of legislating divided between committees, it was soon realised that some further division of labour was going to be necessary if Congress was to function effectively. To meet this demand, subcommittees were created under each committee. Each subcommittee, made up of a small number of members drawn from the ranks of its parent committee, specialises in a narrow area of policy. During the 107th Congress, for instance, the House Committee on

Energy and Commerce divided its work between six subcommittees:

- Subcommittee on Commerce, Trade and Consumer Protection
- Subcommittee on Energy and Air Quality
- Subcommittee on Environment and Hazardous Materials
- Subcommittee on Health
- Subcommittee on Oversight and Investigations
- Subcommittee on Telecommunications and the Internet

This further division of labour allows these small panels of legislators and their staff to devote their time and resources in order to gain enough knowledge to write effective legislation. As will be discussed later, the position of subcommittees within Congress has also become a matter of Congressional politics as well as practicality.

Committee hearings

Once a bill, or several bills on the same topic have been referred to a committee for consideration, they will be handed down to the relevant subcommittee who will carry out the bulk of the work. The first job of the subcommittee is to research the issue; this is done by holding *hearings*.

Hearings are sessions of a subcommittee (or committee) where witnesses from a variety of backgrounds are invited to give their opinion and answer questions on the current law or proposed legislation. Exactly who is invited to give evidence is entirely in the hands of the committee, but most hearings have a familiar cast of participants. The committee will ensure it takes testimony from the executive department or agency with responsibility for the area of policy under consideration, representatives of any group, industry or workforce who are likely to be affected by the policy and pressure groups with an interest in the issue. Individuals can also appear before the committee, whether they be elected officials (e.g. members of Congress with a interest in the topic, state governors, city mayors or other local officials), respected experts in the area or ordinary citizens who find themselves affected by the law.

The primary function of hearings is to allow the committee members to gain enough knowledge to determine whether a change in the law is necessary, and if it is, what the details of the new law should be. Hearings, however, also serve several other purposes. They allow groups with a stake in the issue to get their voice heard, which not only allow the groups to feel they are not being excluded from the political process but also to ensure that America's laws have a democratic basis. Hearings ensure that those members who will ultimately write the law are, at least in theory, exposed to a wide spectrum of opinions and arguments to help them make their own minds up, preventing a blinkered approach. They can also alert members of Congress to how proposals will be received by the public. Finally, the hearings have a public relations element to them, allowing the committee to demonstrate that they are taking their job seriously, that they have done their research and subsequently any legislation which they present to Congress can be trusted to do the job it claims.

To what extent groups or individuals can actually shape the content of legislation by appearing at hearings is a matter for debate. It can be argued that it is unlikely that committee members, who have often debated the key issues over a number of years, will have their mind changed by the arguments or evidence presented by a group or individual. Members of Congress have often committed themselves to a particular course of action or stated a position on the issue during previous election campaigns or Congressional debates. Evidence about a problem which needs to be addressed in itself does not bring with it a universally agreed solution, as with much in politics, answers are a matter of opinion. Evidence, for instance, that America's oil supplies are running low could lead a legislator to conclude that either further regulation of drilling by oil companies is necessary to protect the dwindling resources or that deregulation is necessary to encourage the discovery of new reserves; two opposite conclusions. The accusation is that the point of view of a committee member will be more affected by politics and the interests of their voters than by the merits of the debate during a hearing. In short, it is argued, members do not approach this stage of the legislative process with an open mind.

Despite such arguments, there is evidence that such hearings do have an impact on the final shape of legislation. While they will rarely prompt legislators to do a u-turn on strongly held and publicly-stated beliefs, the exact detail of a proposed law is frequently far from settled. Hearings 'flag-up' particular problems or issues which may previously have been ignored. They can present alternative solutions to problems which may have not been considered and, if the committee is split on the issue, there is a chance to sway the votes of those members who previously had little interest in the particular issue.

Mark-up

Once the subcommittee has completed its hearings it will move to *mark-up*, that is, to write the detail of the legislation. Amendments to the proposals on the table can be offered by any of the members for a vote by the subcommittee as a whole. Line by line, the bill will be agreed, if not by all, by a majority of the subcommittee. It will then face a final vote before being reported back to its parent committee.

Once the bill has been reported to full committee, it will go through another mark-up at committee level. This gives members not on the subcommittee a chance to offer amendments, and those members on the subcommittee who were unsuccessful in the previous mark-up, to try and get their proposals adopted by the full committee. Once amendments have been offered and the final bill agreed, it is reported out of committee to be placed on the waiting list for debate and final passage.

The importance of the committee stages of the legislative process should not be underestimated. In many ways it is the committees which determine the agenda of Congress. The *gate-keeping* function gives committees the power to determine which legislation makes it on to the schedule of the House or Senate for final passage. The committee and subcommittees determine their own agenda, if they decide that an issue is not a priority, it is unlikely that any bills referred to them for consideration will reach even the hearing stage during that Congress. Even if hearings are held on an issue, the committee or subcommittee can still decide not to proceed with legislation. This is exactly what happened with President Clinton's much heralded healthcare reforms in 1993.

Aside from the gate-keeping function, the committees are also the primary arena for framing the bills which eventually become law. While it is the whole of the House and Senate which ultimately determine America's federal laws – they have the final power to amend, reject or pass legislation – it is the committees that writes the legislation which is the basis for debate, and consequently have a major input into the form of the final law.

Committee selection

If a member wishes to influence federal policy to aid them in pursuit of their goals (discussed in chapter 2), they will be at a disadvantage if they do not have a seat on the committee which deals with the issue of most importance to them. The process of committee selection is in the hands of each party, in particular the party leadership.

At the start of each Congress, the first job of the Republican and Democrat leaders in the House or Senate is to agree the proportion of seats each party will be allowed on the various committees. While in theory the party with a majority in either House or Senate could force through their own wishes, it has become convention that the party balance of the committees is agreed between the leaderships and is roughly comparable to the ratio of Republicans and Democrats in the chamber as a whole. Once the number of members from each party on each committee has been agreed, the process begins of assigning members to those seats.

One of the first jobs for new members of Congress is to supply the steering committee of their party with a request list of the committees they wish to take a seat on. Members returning to Congress after re-election (or, in the case of some Senators simply returning to continue their six-year term) can usually expect to keep their previous assignments, but they can also request to be transferred between committees. The Democrat or Republican steering committees, headed by the party leaderships, understand the importance of gaining the right committee assignments to their members' ability to serve their constituents and aid re-election, and will do their best to accommodate as many requests as they can. However, how far any one request can be satisfied will depend on a number of factors.

The most significant restriction on the ability of members to gain a seat on the committee or committees of their choice is the number of vacant seats available. Vacancies on committees occur through members who had previously held a seat not returning to the new Congress (either thorough retirement or failing to gain re-election), returning members moving committee or through the expansion of the number of seats held by one of the parties. Even where there are vacancies, some committees are considered more desirable than others and consequently the parties will regularly receive more requests for seats on these than there are places available. To this end, the rules of the House and Senate categorise the committees as to their importance, and restrict the number of committees a member can sit on according to category (see Box 4.2). In the House, seats on the most important committees are rarely given to new members and as such must be 'earned' by competent service over a period of time. As we will see in chapter 5, this process gives both party leaderships a limited ability to reward or punish members for their behaviour.

Bias in committees?

The process of assigning seats to members has led to accusations that the membership of certain committees, in terms of their views on the issues contained within their committee's jurisdiction, are not representative of the House or Senate as a whole. In political science terminology, certain committees have a *policy bias*. If this is true, it must be a matter of concern considering the influence committees potentially have over the content of legislation. Are America's federal laws being shaped by small groups of politicians whose views are not necessarily representative of Congress as a whole? There are two central competing theories.

Box 4.2   Classification of committees

The rules of the House restrict members from sitting on more than two full committees and four subcommittees. Four committees (Appropriations; Commerce; Rules; Ways and Means) are classified as 'exclusive'; members on one of these committees cannot hold any other assignments. Some of the remaining committees are classified as 'major' by the parties, and restrict members to sitting on only one major committee at a time (although they may also hold a seat on a non-major committee). The exact classification of these and the restriction applied varies between the parties.

The rules of the Senate classify committees as either 'A', 'B' or 'C'. Generally, Senators can serve on no more than two 'A' committees and one 'B' committee; they may, however, be also assigned a seat on a 'C' committee.

'A' committees
Agriculture, Nutrition and
   Forestry
Appropriations
Armes Services
Banking Housing and Urban
   Affairs
Commerce, Science and
   Transportation
Energy and Natural Resources
Environment and Public
   Works
Finance
Government Affairs
Foreign Relations
Health, Education, Labor and
   Pensions

'B' committees
Budget
Rules and Administration
Veterans' Affairs
Joint Economic Committee

'C' committees
Ethics
Indian Affairs
Joint Committee on Taxation

The *distributive* theory of committees argues that bias in committees does indeed exist. Under this model, the purpose of committees is to help individual members achieve their goals by allowing them to become involved in areas of policy of most concern to their constituents. Take the example of Terry Everett, Republican Representative for Alabama's second district. First elected in 1992, the son of a former sharecropper, Everett represents a district dominated by two industries: farming and defence. Everett's district produces more peanuts than almost any other area in the United States and contains the US Air Force's Air University at Maxwell Air Force Base, the Army's Aviation Warfighting Centre at Fort Rucker and a large missile assembly plant in rural Pike County. It should come as no surprise that in order to serve his constituents effectively and to aid his own re-election Everett sought, and received, assignments to both the Agriculture and Armed Services committees of the House. In addition he formed the House Peanut Caucus and serves on the Speciality Crops subcommittee (of the Agriculture committee) which deals with peanuts.

Terry Everett is, of course, not alone in requesting committee assignments which meet his representation and re-election needs. Indeed it would be illogical for a representative whose district covers, say, New York City, to seek a placement on the Agriculture committee. It is also in the interests of the party leaderships to ensure that, as far as possible, their members receive committee assignments which will go some way towards aiding their re-election. Accordingly, the result of this process is that committees are accused of being unrepresentative of Congress as a whole; that, for example, the Agriculture committee, consisting of members of Congress from districts dominated by farming and farmers, will not necessarily legislate in the interests of the nation as a whole.

This analysis is not accepted by everyone. The *informational* model, originally developed by Keith Krehbiel, argues that it would be folly for Congress to allow itself to be dominated by small groups of unrepresentative legislators, making laws only in the interests of their constituents. Ultimately, all laws must be approved by a majority of both House and Senate. Each member who votes for a piece of legislation faces the possibility of that decision being scrutinised by opponents in a future election, especially if the law they helped approve turns out to have negative results or unexpected side-effects for their own constituents. Accordingly, it is not in the interest of the parties or Congress as a whole to allow their committees to become dominated by members with atypical views or to pass legislation which would benefit the few at the cost of the many.

Under the informational model, the job of a committee is not to provide benefits to its own members (although this may still happen), but to act as the 'brains' of Congress. No member can be an expert on all issues, especially as legislation is frequently technically complex. Members want to be assured that the laws they are casting their votes for are well-researched and will not have any major unforeseen negative consequences. The committees are the way in which the House and Senate delegate the job of researching and formulating legislation, to try and ensure that the legislation which is eventually passed has a sound basis and will complete the job it sets out to do. In short, the committees are the servants of Congress and it not in the interests of the House or Senate as a whole for them to become unrepresentative units solely looking after their own interests.

The truth is probably somewhere between these two competing theories. Whatever the reality of how representative committees are of Congress as a whole, is it still true that if a member wishes to hold significant influence over an area of policy, a seat on the relevant committee is still vital.

Power within the committee

Not all committee members however will have an equal say over all areas of policy under their jurisdiction. Much of this distribution of influence is down to self-selection. Even with a committee place secured, if a member wishes to gain influence in a particular policy area, it will still take a significant investment of their resources to gather the expertise and commit the time necessary to become fully involved. It is not practical, and probably not desirable, for a member to attempt to become an expert in all areas of a committee's policy. Consequently, members will pick and choose which policies they wish to concentrate on.

However, power within committees is primarily distributed on formal lines. The most powerful member of any one committee is the *chair*. Under a process known as *seniority*, this position is usually held by the member of the majority party who has served the longest on the committee, with their counterpart in the opposing party known as the *ranking minority member*. Until the 1970s, committee chairs were more or less all-powerful. They controlled the committee staff and budget, could determine when and where the committee gathered for hearings, which issues made it onto the agenda and had the power to determine the number and nature of their committee's subcommittees. Chairs would also assume the power of voting by *proxy*, that is casting the votes of members of their own party who were absent from any committee meeting. Some of the more determined chairs became notorious for using their powers to maintain a vice-like grip over the policies under their committee's jurisdiction.

Changes in the rules and procedures of Congress, especially in the House (discussed below), has meant that committee chairs have had their influence curtailed. However, the committee chair is still the most powerful member of the committee. They still have a great deal of control over the allocation of committee staff and resources, the scheduling of committee hearings and the general shape of the committee agenda. Aside from these institutional powers, the committee chairs gain much of their influence because of their position of leadership and experience. The committee chairs, as leader of the majority party on their committee will be active in negotiating to form the coalitions needed to pass legislation and as a matter of course will be involved in the major legislation under their jurisdiction. Having spent enough time on the committee to rise to the position of leadership, the committee chairs often have a great deal of knowledge and experience of the issues to buttress their power.

Power over the floor

For all the advantages of the committee in writing legislation and the power of the committee chair to impose their will on the committee, it would be for nothing if the legislation emerging from the committee is not passed into law. For any bill to become law it must be passed by majority vote on the floor of both the House and Senate. The aim of any committee must be to not only ensure that the legislation it reports passes a vote by their parent chamber, but that it is passed without significant amendment. Committees possess a number of informal powers to help them achieve this aim.

The first informal power is linked to the informational model of committees, discussed above. We showed how members need to be sure that the laws they vote for will not have any unexpected side-effect. Members also want to be sure that the policies they approve are good ones; that they have been well-researched and carefully formulated. This is especially true in areas which are technically complex and perhaps foreign to most non-committee members. Members may disagree with the aim of the law and vote against it, but when they do vote in favour of a piece of legislation, they need to have confidence that the committee has done a good job, that the legislation will effectively achieve its stated goal. As Krehbiel argues 'committees earn the compliance of their parent chamber by convincing the chamber that what the committee wants is in the chamber's interest'.[1]

Consequently, committees who earn a reputation for expertly researching their legislation will often find that non-committee members are more likely to trust their judgement and pass the laws without significant amendment. Richard Fenno illustrates this point by quoting a prominent House leader who spoke about one House committee in glowing terms, 'The Committee has a very good reputation. I think the Committee is accepted as doing work of high standards. They present their bills well. They are very seldom amended on the floor . . . You know they have gone through it with a fine-tooth comb'.[2] In this way, committees that establish a reputation for drafting well-researched legislation will have enhanced the chances of their bills surviving the scrutiny of a floor debate and becoming law.

A second power which is often attributed to committees appears as a result of what has become known as *log-rolling*.[3] Under this process, it is argued, a trade takes place between the various committees to allow passage of committee bills. Non-committee members will, except in situations of extreme uncertainty over a proposal, defer to a committee's findings in the expectation that their own committee's reports will be treated with the same respect. Any member daring to upset this arrangement may run the risk that proposals emanating from their own committee, in which they have a greater interest, will face similar opposition. Any losses, in terms of policy preferences, suffered by a legislator will be made up for in the long term by gains in the areas of most importance to them.[4]

The degree to which log-rolling allows committees to see the policies they prefer pass into law is debatable. It would be a mistake to assume that committees have free rein to determine the content of legislation which passes Congress. During floor debates legislation is frequently amended and is occasionally defeated. However, it is also true that by determining the bill which forms the basis of the debate and by holding an advantage in terms of expertise, committees are in an advantageous position to influence the final outcome.

The extent to which committees can impose their will on the House or Senate can depend on the nature of the committee itself. As the quote supplied by Fenno (above) indicates, a committee which has earned a reputation for approaching its task professionally and producing reliable legislation will find it easier to persuade the rest of the House or Senate to support its bill. Such reputations can depend on whether the committee is in agreement. Legislation with the unanimous support of committee members is more likely to inspire confidence in non-committee members who may have little knowledge of the issue than a bill over which committee members disagree. This is especially true if disagreements between committee members continue during the floor debate. The ability of the committee to use its superior knowledge to persuade non-members to support their legislation will be damaged if the committee itself cannot agree on what is the best way forward. Consequently, a divided committee usually leads to divisions in the rest of the House or Senate when it comes to the floor debate. If the committee is divided along party lines, then the shape of the floor debate will often mirror that split. It is important then for a committee to work to accommodate its own members if it wants to ensure its bills make the final journey into law.

Perhaps the greatest difficulty committees face in turning their bills into law is simply that for a law to be made, any proposal must gain the approval of both the House of Representatives and the Senate and run the gauntlet of a pos- sible presidential veto. While, say, the House Committee on Health may research and draft legislation on healthcare for senior citizens, and using their position within the chamber, succeed in persuading the House of Representatives to approve the measure, it cannot become law unless the Senate also agrees. To this end, it is important for House committees to maintain a dialogue with their Senate equivalent, and vice versa.

Can the House or Senate control their committees?
Theoretically, while committees hold a great deal of power, final authority within Congress lies with the House or Senate as a whole. Decisions made by a committee or by the party leaderships can be overturned by a vote of the full chamber. The number of seats allocated to the parties on each commit- tee and which members fill those seats are both decisions which require ratification by a vote of the full chamber. However, in reality, members rarely choose to exercise this power and such votes go through as a formality.

Another device designed to check the power of committees available in the House of Representatives is the *discharge*

petition. If a committee is refusing to act on a piece of legislation, the House can force the committee to report the measure
by issuing a petition. However, with the petition needing the
signatures of a majority of House members (currently 218),
they are very rarely successful. Members are often reluctant
to interfere with a committee's work fearing that the use of
such devices may lead to their own committee facing similar
challenges. Since 1967, only 11 such petitions have gained the
necessary signatures. The discharge petition was used effectively in 2002 over the issue of campaign finance reform (see
Box 4.3).

The area in which the House of Representatives has been
successful in curtailing their committees is the power of the
chair (the Senate, in contrast have few formal rules on such
matters). During the 1960s the Democrats controlled the
House, but the powerful committee chairmen were becoming
increasingly out of step with the wishes of the majority of
Democrats on issues including civil rights. This was due to an
anomaly in American politics whereby conservative Democrats from the southern states had served for a longer period
than any of their more moderate party colleagues and accordingly had risen to positions of authority within the committee
system through the rule of seniority. In the 1970s, frustrated
by the obstructionist nature of the committee chairs, the
House Democrats succeeded in pushing through a number of
reforms which limited the chairs' power.

One of the reformers first actions was to challenge the convention of seniority. The Democrat Caucus (which includes all
Democrat members) in the House voted to give subcommittees greater autonomy from their full committee chair. In
1971, in an attempt to share power more widely, the Democrat Caucus adopted a rule whereby no Democrat House

Box 4.3   The battle for campaign finance

In July 2001 the House of Representatives gathered to debate a bill which would tighten the rules governing political donations. In particular it looked to bring so-called 'soft money' (donations to parties, rather than directly to candidates) under the law. A similar bill had already passed the Senate and so if the House did likewise, there was a good chance of the reforms becoming law.

It quickly became clear that the House's approval was going to be hard fought, especially as the Republican leadership was opposed to the measure. The first battle was to be over the rule, which set the terms of debate. The main sponsors of the bill, Christopher Shays and Martin Meehan wished to introduce some amendments, planned to broaden support for it. However, under the proposed rule, rather than allow a single vote on the changes, the Republican leadership were insisting, through the rule, that separate votes must be taken on each measure, a total of 14. Supporters of the bill charged that the rule was designed purely to make it as difficult as possible for Shays and Meehan to see their changes passed, and thus undermine support for the bill as a whole. When the rule was put to a vote, enough Republicans defied their leadership and voted with the majority of Democrats to see it defeated. With no rule, there could be no debate. During angry exchanges, the Republican leadership announced that they had no plans to bring another rule to the floor in the near future, effectively dooming the bill to failure.

Supporters of the measure were not giving up. With the unfolding scandals surrounding the collapse of Enron Corporation and questions being asked about the effect of political donations by the company, the fate of the campaign finance bill remained a high-profile issue. By January 2002, the Democrat leadership had managed to gather the signatures of 218 House members (including a number of Republicans) on a discharge petition. This success meant that they could present the petition and force the bill back onto the floor of the House. It was the use of this device that was instrumental in seeing the campaign finance bill finally become law.

member could chair more than one subcommittee. Two years later, a raft of proposals which became known as the 'subcommittee bill of rights' were adopted and further strengthened in 1974. The power of committee chairs was limited by so-called 'sunshine' rules that ensured that most meetings were now guaranteed to be open to the public and also prevented the chair from sometimes holding no meetings at all. The proposals also strengthened the position of subcommittees by taking the power to choose who would chair each subcommittee away from the full committee chair and allowing all Democrat committee members to vote on the matter. Subcommittees were strengthened further by being given control over their own staff.

The transformation of the role of the subcommittee in the House of Representatives led to political scientists Roger Davidson and Walter Oleszek adapting Woodrow Wilson's characterisation of 'Congressional government as committee government', instead describing it as *subcommittee* government. The reforms succeeded in limiting the power of committee chairs and created an environment where more junior representatives could become effectively involved in the policy-making process and rise to positions of authority in a relatively short period of time.

Republican reforms in the 104th Congress

The Constitution of the United States laid out the principle that the House of Representatives and the Senate can determine their own rules. The reality of politics, especially in the House, has meant that this power is in the hands of the majority party. Consequently, when the Republican Party took control of the House of Representatives in 1995, it was unsurprising that the leadership, and in particular, Speaker Newt

Gingrich should make their own changes to the committee system. These changes have gone some way towards reversing the impact of the Democrat reforms of the 1970s.

As Gingrich saw it, the problem with the committee system in the House was twofold. Firstly, the number of committees allowed (and indeed encouraged) members to pursue their individual projects and gather pork barrel for their districts without any restraint or thought for the greater national need. Secondly, the autonomy of committees and subcommittees prevented the party leadership from being able to pursue a policy agenda for the nation as a whole. This was a particularly pertinent point considering the commitment the Republican leadership had to the *Contract with America*.

The reforms passed by the new Republican majority in 1995 took away many of the advantages held by the subcommittees, but ensured that power did not simply revert to the full committee and its chair. In order to reverse the trend of decentralisation of power within the House, the number of committees and subcommittees were reduced. Under the Gingrich reforms, three full committees were abolished,[5] and in the majority of cases the number of subcommittees a committee was entitled to was restricted to five. The autonomy of subcommittees was limited with control of all committee staff being placed under the command of the full committee chair, taking away the power of the subcommittee leader and ranking minority member to appoint one member of staff each. However, the full committees suffered as well, seeing the total number of committee staff throughout the House cut by one-third. Individual members were restricted to serving on two full committees and four subcommittees, and any chair of a committee or subcommittee were limited to serving three consecutive terms in that post.

By limiting the amount of committees one member could serve on and by ensuring a limited tenure for chairs, the Republican leadership hoped to prevent members from building their own personal power bases from where they could challenge the authority of the party leadership. To check the ability of individual members to pursue their own ends further, all committee and subcommittee meetings were to be held in public (unless doing so would threaten national security), the details of every vote cast by each member were to be published and the casting of proxy votes by the chair was outlawed.

The changes which the Republicans made were a direct attempt to limit the ability of committees to pursue their own ends at the expense of the party leadership. Within their own party, changes were also made to make full committee chairs responsible to, and removable by, the party as a whole. Indeed one of the first actions Newt Gingrich took on assuming the Speaker's chair was to ensure that three senior Republicans who would have risen to the position of committee chair under the norm of seniority were replaced by more junior members who were ideologically acceptable to Gingrich. In short, the purpose of the 1995 Republican reforms was to swing the pendulum of power away from the committee and subcommittee towards the party leadership, but with only limited success.

Assessing the role of committees

The power of committees in Congress has regularly come under fire by politicians and commentators alike. Particular criticism has been reserved for their part in what has been described as '*subgovernments*' or '*iron triangles*'. The argument put forward is that in any one policy area the relevant

Congressional committee, executive branch department or agency and interested pressure groups reach agreement and use their position within government to dictate policy. On leaving office in 1960, President Eisenhower (himself a former General) warned of the dangers of such subgovernments in the area of military spending, or what he termed the 'military-industrial complex'. Eisenhower argued that the power of the presidency was thwarted by the combination of bureaucrats and military leaders in the executive branch, Congressional committees with jurisdiction over defence issues and arms manufacturers, all who had an interest in increasing defence spending for their own ends.

The validity of this argument has, however, been questioned since. Hugh Heclo, for one, has argued that such rigid subgovernments reaching agreement over the direction of policy are very hard to achieve. The number of actors involved in any one policy area are often great, making agreement very difficult to reach. Indeed, proliferation in the number of interest groups since the 1970s has led to a situation whereby, in any policy area, a diversity of opinions is almost guaranteed. Even where there is agreement over the goals which should be pursued, there will frequently be disagreement over the means or the detail of the policy.

To whatever extent the power of committees has been diluted or effected by changes since the 1970s, it is clear that, within the federal government, Congressional committees are still the primary arena in terms of policy formulation. Just as President Clinton discovered with his Health Care plan, committees hold the power to kill, pass or rewrite any legislation which comes to them. Even though the full chamber of the House or Senate officially holds the final authority, in reality, the power of committee is still a formidable one.

Summary

Committees and their subcommittees are the engine rooms of the House and Senate. They are the arenas in which legislation is researched and written before going to the full chamber for debate. Committees also act as the gate-keepers of Congress, the place where most legislation will die. Members of Congress generally request committee assignments which will give them influence over issues which will aid them in achieving their goals of re-election and good public policy. This has led to accusations that committees are often not representative of the views of Congress as a whole. This could be important considering that committees do have a certain degree of informal power over their full chamber when it comes to the passage of legislation, although this can vary between committees and between issues. Within the committee power is not distributed evenly, with the chair holding the most influence.

Notes

1 K. Krehbiel, *Information and Legislative Organization* (Ann Arbor: University of Michigan Press 1991), p. 256.
2 R. F. Fenno Jr., *Congressmen in Committees* (Boston: Little Brown, 1973), p. 198.
3 The equivalent term in the UK would be 'back-scratching'.
4 R. Axelrod, *The Evolution of Cooperation* (New York: Basic Books, 1984).
5 District of Columbia, Merchant Marine and Fisheries, and Post Office and Civil Service.

Parties in Congress

> The Democrats are the party of government activism, the
> party that says government can make you richer, smarter,
> taller, and get the chickweed out of your lawn. Republicans
> are the party that says government doesn't work, and then
> get elected and prove it. (P. J. O'Rourke)

One of the most often overlooked aspects of Congress is the
role played by political parties. It is true that parties in the
United States are weaker and more fragmented than many of
their Western European counterparts. It is also true that the
majority of members of Congress cannot rely on their party
label alone to assure their election and instead must develop
their own platform and reputation. However, it is a fact that
since 1945 only a handful of candidates for Congress have
successfully gained election without the official endorsement
of one of the two major parties. Consequently, parties are still
of vital importance in Congress and deserve fuller understanding.

Organisation by party

On 24 May 2001, Senator Jim Jeffords of Vermont, in
a statement he called his 'declaration of independence',

announced that 'In order to best represent my state of
Vermont, my own conscience, and the principles I have stood
for my whole life, I leave the Republican Party and become
an Independent'. Jeffords was not the first sitting member of
Congress to defect from the party under whose banner they
were elected. Indeed, since 1981 there have been sixteen
party defections in Congress, although, before Jeffords, only
one from the Republican Party in that time. What made
Jefford's decision so notable, was that his actions changed the
balance of power in the Senate. The results of the 2000 election had left the Senate divided between fifty Democrats and
fifty Republicans. Jefford's defection, placed the Senate in the
hands of the Democrats.

Congress is organised along party lines. The leaders of the
Democrat and Republican Parties in the House of Representatives and Senate hold key positions in their chamber with
power over the legislative agenda, the organisation of
Congress and matters such as members' committee assignments. The largest share of this power is reserved for the leadership of the *majority party*. The main leadership posts are
outlined in Box 5.1 and their roles are outlined below.

Party leaders in the House of Representatives

Speaker of the House

Party politics aside, the Speaker is an extremely important
figure in the Government of the United States, being second
only to the Vice-President in the line of succession to the presidency. Within the House itself the Speaker is the presiding
officer, referring bills to committees, presiding over debates
and judging points of order. These roles occasionally afford
the Speaker a great deal of influence over the fate of legisla-

Box 5.1   Party leadership in the 107th Congress

Majority party	*Minority party*
House of Representatives	
Republicans	*Democrats*
Speaker of the House: Dennis Hastert	No equivalent post for the minority party
Majority Leader: Richard Armey	Minority Leader: Richard Gephardt
Majority Whip: Tom Delay	Minority Whip: Nancy Pelosi
Republican Conference Chair: J. C. Watts	House Democratic Caucus Chair: Martin Frost
Republican Policy Committee Chair: Chris Cox	Democratic Policy Committee Vice-Chairs: *Several*
Senate	
Democrats	*Republicans*
Majority Leader: Tom Daschle	Minority Leader: Trent Lott
Assistant Majority Leader (Democrat Whip): Harry Reid	Assistant Minority Leader (Republican Whip): Don Nickles
Democrat Policy Committee Chair: Byron Dorgan	Republican Policy Committee Chair: Larry Craig
No Democrat equivalent	Republican Conference Chair: Rick Santorum

tion, but in reality, for most of the time, such duties are formalities and as such are carried out by assistants. The power of the modern Speaker is derived partly from the institutional position and duties and partly from his other role, that of leader of the majority party in the House. In this role the Speaker has a great deal of influence over the pursuit of his party's legislative agenda. He is a central figure in deciding legislative priorities, determining committee assignments, accommodating members' requests and, through the Rules Committee (discussed below) the agenda of the House as a whole. He will act as the party's spokesman and chief nego- tiator with the minority party leaders, the Senate and the President. While any leader of the party has few official sanc- tions to bring rogue members into line, the importance of the post of Speaker and his central position in the party's 'com- munication network' gives the office holder a great deal of influence to dispense favours and persuade members with the aim of forming the coalitions necessary to get legislation passed.

Ultimately, the power of the Speaker will depend on the ability of the office holder. Over the years, some speakers have used the tools at their disposal to great effect. Legendary speakers in the history of the House include 'uncle' Joe Cannon (speaker, 1903–11) and Sam Rayburn (1940–47, 1949–53, 1955–63) who were noted for the power with which they brought to the post of Speaker. As discussed in chapter 4, Newt Gingrich (1995–99) attempted to use his position within the Republican Party and Congress as a whole to concentrate power of the legislative agenda in the Speaker's chair. How far he succeeded will be discussed below.

Majority Leader

The Majority Leader acts as deputy to the Speaker. His role, however, is more 'hands-on' than the Speaker. The Majority Leader is in charge of guiding legislation through the floor debates, negotiating with minority party members and build- ing coalitions to pass the majority party's legislative prior- ities.

Minority Leader

There is no minority party equivalent to the Speaker of the House. Instead, the Minority Leader must play the leadership roles of both the Speaker and Majority Leader within his own party. The Minority Leader plays a central role in setting the minority's legislative priorities, negotiating with the majority and with the White House, assigning members to committees and building coalitions to pass or defeat legislation on the floor.

Majority Whip

The Majority Whip has the job of marshalling the rank and file of the majority party. He acts as a link between the leaders and party members in Congress, gathering information on members' voting intentions, persuading members to follow the party line and providing information about forthcoming votes and the leadership's legislative priorities.

Minority Whip

The Minority Whip performs the same functions for the minority as the Majority Whip does for the majority.

Republican Conference Chair

The Republican Conference contains all Republican members in the House who then elect the chair. The chair acts as a spokesman for the party, a mediator between Republicans where there are sharp policy disagreements, and as a disciplinarian of members who consistently defy the party line. The conference as a whole is also the arena where leadership elections take place and where disputes over internal Republican matters are finally settled.

Democratic Caucus Chair
The Democratic Caucus and its chair perform the same role for the Democrats as the Conference does for the Republicans.

Republican Policy Committee Chair
The Republican Policy Committee has the job of analysing legislative proposals and recommending strategy to the party. It also produces briefing papers to help members in answering questions from the public and the press.

Democratic Policy Committee Vice-Chairs
The Democratic Policy Committee and its vice-chairs perform the same role as the Republican Policy Committee.

Party leaders in the Senate

Senate Majority Leader
The leader and main spokesman of the majority party in the Senate. The Majority Leader manages the day-to-day business on the Senate floor, working with committee leaders, scheduling floor debates and setting legislative priorities.

Senate Assistant Majority Leader
The Assistant Majority Leader performs a similar function to the *Majority Whip* in the House. The job entails keeping party members informed of upcoming issues and working to build coalitions to ensure that the legislation supported by the party pass on the floor of the Senate.

Senate Minority Leader
The Senate Minority Leader is the head of the minority party and fulfils the equivalent role of the Senate Majority Leader.

Senate Minority Whip
The Senate Minority Whip is the minority party equivalent to the Assistant Majority Leader.

Senate Republican Conference
The Senate Republican Conference is the meeting of all Republican Senators and acts as a forum where party leaders and rank-and-file members can meet and discuss their concerns.

Senate Republican Policy Committee
The Committee and its chair is charged with developing policy and legislative strategy.

Senate Democratic Conference Secretary
The third-ranking Democrat Senator, the Democratic Conference Secretary oversees the Conference which performs the equivalent role for Democrats as the Republican Conference.

Senate Democratic Policy Committee
The Senate Democratic Policy Committee performs the equivalent role to the Republican Policy Committee.

The power of party leaders

A common caricature of parties in the United States is of loose organisations with little ability to control or even choose the elected officials who represent them. To a certain extent this is true; as was discussed in chapter 2, the diversity of the nation and the primary election system has led to members of Congress having a great deal of autonomy from their party. However, leaders attempt to use the limited powers at their disposal to keep the party in line.

Leadership styles

The 'power to persuade' is normally associated with the President, but it is no less important to party leaders in Congress. With few official sanctions available to discipline members, the success of a leader in controlling the party often depends on their personal diplomatic skills. Cajoling, persuading and negotiating with members in order to form voting coalitions is an essential part of a leader's job. Different leaders have used different approaches to achieve this end, with varying results.

One of the most successful leaders in this way was Lyndon B. Johnson, Senate Majority Leader from 1955 to 1960. Johnson used his intellect, presence and sheer physical size to persuade or even bully Senators into supporting the party's position. This became known as 'the treatment' and was described by Rowland Evans and Robert Novak thus:

> The tone was supplication, accusation, cajolery, exuberance, scorn, tears, complaint, the hint of threat. It was all these together. It ran the gamut of human emotions. Its velocity was breathtaking, and it was all in one direction. Interjections from the target were rare. Johnson anticipated them before they could be spoken. He moved in close, his face a scant millimetre from his target, his eyes widening and narrowing, his eyebrows rising and falling. From his pockets poured clippings, memos, statistics. Mimicry, humour, and the genius of analogy made The Treatment an almost hypnotic experience and rendered the target stunned and helpless . . .[1]

As Evans and Novak suggest, LBJ's success was not simply due to intimidation. Party leaders hold advantage over other members of their party due to their knowledge of the issues and Congressional procedures. This is partly accrued through the length of service in Congress which leaders inevitably have, but also through the party's communication network. Leaders need to keep their finger on the pulse of the whole range of legislative activity within their domain.

Bob Dole, Senate Majority Leader 1985–87 and 1995–96, and Minority Leader 1987–95, was more of a coalition builder than LBJ, but like Johnson he also relied on an encyclopaedic knowledge of the legislative process. Senator Mark Hatfield, who worked closely with Dole, described his leadership style thus:

> First of all, he is an information gatherer. In other words, he has to know where different members of the Senate are coming from . . . maybe he has enough Republican votes to pass something. But if he doesn't . . . then he has to move across the aisle, and find out who on that side of the aisle he can bring together with those Republicans to pass a bill. Now that's the role of the majority leader. His style is different than LBJ . . . Senator Dole gathers information . . . I'm not aware that Senator Dole ever threatened . . . And I'm not sure that I have ever heard any one of my colleagues say he'd threatened them . . . Senator Dole is not that type of leader. He's a consensus builder.[2]

Newt Gingrich, House Speaker 1995–98, had a contrasting style to Dole's. Gingrich was more aggressive and partisan. He came to the job on the back of a Republican electoral landslide, and was determined to push through the *Contract with America*. Gingrich personalised the Republican program and the inevitable conflict with the Clinton White House more than any other Speaker. He attempted to centralise power in the Speaker's chair by pushing through changes in the rules of Congress which diminished the autonomy of committees (discussed in chapter 4). With the support of newly elected

Republican members (many of whom initially felt loyalty towards Gingrich for his part in their election), Gingrich persuaded the party to vote to award the chair of three committees to members more sympathetic to his views, passing over the norm of seniority.

Control of the legislative process

As the example of Gingrich suggests, party leaders have more tools at their disposal than simply force of personality. The Constitution states that 'Each House may determine the rules of its proceedings' (Article 1, Section 5); at the start of each Congress, the majority party leaders can propose changes to the way either the House or Senate operated, provided the changes are approved by a majority of Senators or Representatives. In this way, Gingrich instituted changes in the committee system, much as Democrats did in the 1970s. Alternatively, leaders are in an advantageous position to push through changes within their own party which affect their degree of control over the legislative process, as Gingrich did by ensuring committee chairs were inhabited by members who would be sympathetic to his agenda. The leadership also has some influence over who is assigned to which commitee.

The leader of the majority party in the House or Senate also have the power of *referral*. When a bill is introduced it must be referred to a committee for consideration. While this procedure is usually straightforward, there are occasions when it can give the leadership influence. During the 1960s, the Democrat leadership was trying to push civil rights legislation through Congress, but was being thwarted by committee chairmen opposed to the measures. In an attempt to overcome this opposition, the leaderships in House and Senate pursued different strategies regarding committee referral. In the House, the bill was written as to allow the leadership to refer it to the Judiciary Committee, a strategy which increased its chances of success as the committee was chaired by Emanuel Celler, a supporter of civil rights. The Senate leadership was aware that the Judiciary Committee of the Senate was dominated by opponents of civil rights who would kill the bill. Consequently, the leadership delayed any action until the measure had passed the House, which allowed them to take the rare step of not referring the bill to a committee at all. After a vote on the floor, the Senate agreed to consider the House bill without any committee consideration. It was this tactic which facilitated the passage of the groundbreaking Civil Rights Act of 1964.

Since 1974, the Speaker of the House of Representatives has also had the option of *multiple referral*. If the Speaker feels that a bill deals with issues with fall under the jurisdiction of more than one committee, he can send either all or parts of the bill to those committees. This can affect the chances of the whole bill or parts of it surviving the committee process. With different committees having different overall viewpoints, the ability to refer bills to more than one committee gave the Speaker a greater deal of influence over the legislative process than he had before.

Perhaps the greatest of the party leaders' powers is that of scheduling. The ability to influence which issues rise to the top of the Congressional agenda, and which see no action due to time running out. If a bill does not pass into law by the end of the Congress into which it was introduced, it fails and must be re-introduced from the beginning in the following Congress and begin the process again. With many pieces of legislation competing for space on the agenda, it is an important power to be able to influence which issues take priority.

How this works in practice differs between the House of Representatives and the Senate.

House Rules Committee

The House Rules Committee has responsibility for regulating the schedule and debates in the chamber of the House of Representatives. When a committee has completed its work on a bill, it will report the legislation to the Rules Committee for a rule to be issued. The rule sets out the maximum amount of time to be allowed for debate and determines whether amendments are allowed to be offered. Three types of rule exist: an *open* rule allows amendments to be offered on any part of the bill during the debate, a *closed* rule forbids any amendments being offered, dictating that the bill can either be passed or failed in its original form but not altered. Alternatively a *modified* rule allows amendments to be offered on specified parts of the bill, but not on others. Which rule is issued can have a significant effect on the chances of the bill passing into law, or at least, succeeding in its original form.

The power to finally decide when a bill is placed on the Congressional schedule and how the debate will take place is a significant one. Consequently, the rules committee is dominated by the leadership of the two parties. However, as with all issues, power ultimately resides with the House of Representatives as a whole. Rules issued by the committee must be passed by a majority vote in the House to come into effect. In the majority of cases this is a formality, although on occasions can cause controversy. Once the rule has been agreed the bill it is concerned with can then be placed on the House calendar for debate.

Unanimous consent agreements in the Senate

The Senate has no rules committee, however the scheduling and structuring of debates is still a matter for party leaders. Instead of issuing rules, as in the House, the leaders of the Democrats and Republicans will craft what are termed as *unanimous consent agreements*. The agreement will outline when a bill is debated and how long that debate is allowed to continue. It will be put to the Senate and if there is no objection, debate can proceed. The problem with this system is that, as the name suggests, the agreements need unanimous consent and as such can be disrupted by a single Senator. The effects of this will be discussed in the next chapter.

Conference committees

Even after a bill has been debated and passed, party leaders still have an opportunity to influence its fate. As will be discussed in the next chapter, one of the difficulties of a bicameral system is that the House and Senate may not agree on the details of a particular piece of legislation. Even if the same bill survives the committee stages of the two chambers, different amendments may be offered during floor debate. When this situation occurs, and neither chamber seems willing to accept the other's version as a whole, a House-Senate conference committee will be convened to negotiate the differences and produce a final version of the bill. Consequently, the members who sit on this committee have a considerable amount of influence over the final shape of legislation. Changes introduced in committee or during floor debate may disappear from the legislation at the conference stage. Each time a conference committee is convened, it is the party leadership who proposes the membership from their side of Congress. While it is normal for committee members who have been active in the formulation of the bill to be appointed and, ultimately, the full membership House or Senate retains a veto over the appointment process, this procedure can give the party leadership influence over the shape of the final legislation.

Sanctions on maverick members

Party leaders have few sanctions at their disposal with which to bring members into line. Unlike parties in the United Kingdom, they cannot threaten them with the removal of the party label at the next election or offer promotion to the cabinet. The sanctions available to Congressional party leaders are less formal, and are connected to the influence they have over scheduling, agenda setting, coalition building and committee appointments. By providing the appropriate committee appointment, giving legislation priority on the schedule and using their influence to persuade others to move the legislative process along, leaders can aid members in achieving their goals. Assurances of priority for their wishes can be used to persuade a member to follow the party line on an important vote. Similarly, members who persistently ignore party demands could find the leadership somewhat less than enthusiastic in accommodating their requests.

Party unity

The lack of sanctions at the leadership's disposal to control maverick members is only part of the reason why unity between party members in Congress is low. In many cases it is not in the interest of the party to demand all members vote the same way. Leaders are aware of the demands which the desire for re-election place on individual members. When considering how they cast their vote or set their priorities, members must give careful consideration to how their actions will be received by the voters. They are aware that any one vote cast could be turned into an issue by a future opponent in either the primary or general election. Such constituency pressures can differ greatly between members of the same party. It is in the interest of leaders to help their members in their bid for re-election, and understand that the priorities of the party and those of individual constituencies will sometimes conflict.

Party government

The system of separation of powers and the weaknesses in party discipline has meant that any form of *party government*, so common in European legislatures, is extremely difficult to achieve. The Congressional system works on compromise, persuasion and trade-offs. It is near impossible for the majority party in Congress to push through a comprehensive slate of policies. The times in American history where a legislative programme, such as the New Deal in 1934, has succeeded in becoming law, the driving force has been the White House rather than Congressional parties.

When Newt Gingrich became Speaker of the House in 1995, he made a bold attempt at party government. His strategy was based on two threads: the changes in the committee system designed to give more influence to the Speaker, and the *Contract with America*. For many House Republicans, especially those who were first elected in 1994, the *Contract* was seen as having been central to their takeover of Congress and consequently they felt a duty to the voters to ensure the passage of the legislation promised within it. Initially, some members wore laminated copies of the *Contract* around their necks, others referred to it as their 'bible'. Bolstered by the support of new Republican members who attributed to Gingrich a large part in their election, the Speaker attempted to marshal his party to ensure the passage of the party's programme.

This attempt to unify the Republican Party behind a legislative programme was successful to a degree, but its failures highlighted the difficulty in achieving anything approaching party government. The commitment made in the *Contract* was not to pass the proposals into law, but to bring them to a vote on the floor of the House of Representatives within 100 days. The Republicans, filled with determination following the election, fulfilled this pledge. Furthermore, they also succeeded in passing into law legislation concerning Congressional accountability, unfunded mandates and stockholders rights, the latter being passed despite a presidential veto. However, the majority of their proposals never completed the journey into law. Three pieces of legislation suffered at the hands of a presidential veto, an attempt to give the President powers to veto parts of a bill was struck down by the Supreme Court as unconstitutional and a proposal to limit the number of times a Representative could seek re-election was defeated in the House itself. An important stumbling block, however, was the US Senate. Senate Republicans had not signed the *Contract* and did not feel bound to supporting all elements in it. The nature of the Senate is less confrontational than the House and as such allows the party leadership less scope in enforcing a party line.

Once the House had dealt with the provisions contained in the *Contract*, the initial enthusiasm by Republicans for any form of party government subsided. As the time for re-election drew nearer, traditional local political concerns took centre stage. With no publicly issued manifesto to hold members to, the familiar patterns (and difficulties) of party control re-emerged.

Relations between leaders

How smoothly Congress functions can be affected by how well the party leaders can get on. Sometimes this can just be a matter of personality. Before the terrorist attacks of 11 September 2001, politics in the House of Representatives were complicated by the strained relationships between the leaders of the Democrats and Republicans, particularly those between Richard Gephardt and Richard Armey. During the 104th Congress, Democrats attempted to make political capital by demonising House Speaker Newt Gingrich. A similar attempt had been made on Senate leader Thomas Daschle by Republicans in the 107th Congress.

It can also be a matter of party differences. Consequently, a change in which party 'controls' the House or Senate can have a significant effect on the politics of the federal government as a whole. If one party controls the House and their opponents control the Senate, in theory it can make agreement more difficult to reach. However, this should not be overstated, as discussed above, the *Contract with America* ran into problems in the Senate, despite the Republicans holding a majority in both chambers. On the other hand, Congress managed to pass often controversial campaign finance reform in 2002, despite the House being controlled by Republicans and the Senate by the Democrats.

Summary

While parties in the United States are weaker than their Western European equivalents, they still play a major role in Congress. Which party controls the House or Senate makes a big difference to the politics of Capitol Hill. The party with a majority will dominate the committees and have a major say over which issues make it onto the Congressional agenda. The party leaders have the most influence over the legislative process, although they are limited in the formal sanctions they have at their disposal to control their own party members. Consequently, achieving any form of 'party government' can prove difficult.

Notes

1 R. Evans and R. Novak, *Lyndon B. Johnson: The Exercise of Power* (The New American Library, Inc., 1966), p. 104.
2 Senator Mark Hatfield, PBS *Frontline*, 10 July 1996.

6

Floor deliberations and beyond

The motion to lay on the table the motion to reconsider the vote by which the motion to lay on the table the motion to proceed to the consideration of the fair housing bill was rejected was agreed to. (Proceedings of the Senate, Congressional Record, 4 December 1980)

To the general public, the most visible parts of Congress are the debates which take place on the floor of the chambers of the House of Representatives and the Senate. Debates are televised live and can contain moments of great controversy and excitement. The most extreme incident took place during a debate in the chamber of the House of Representatives on 1 March 1954. As a quorum count was taking place of the 243 members present at that time, two men and a woman sitting in the public gallery jumped to their feet, and shouting 'Free Puerto Rico', pulled out Luger automatics and opened fire on the members below. Five Representatives were hit; all survived but the injuries left Alabama's Kenneth Roberts in a wheelchair for the next two years.

Most debates, however, are much more sedate. Indeed, visitors to Congress are often surprised by how few members are present during a typical debate. For low profile issues, or those which are technically complex, debates often take place with only a handful of members present. This situation can change suddenly; when a vote is called or a quorum count is to be held, a bell is rung in the Capitol Building and surrounding offices and members pour through the corridors and the tunnels which connect their offices to Congress into the chamber.

Floor debate

The chambers of the House and Senate are where all legislation begins its life and, for the bills which have survived the committee stages, where they complete their Congressional journey. Floor debates are the showpieces of Congress, but much of their business is procedural and mundane. Each morning both the House and Senate start the day with a prayer and, since 1989, the House has followed the prayer with members reciting the Pledge of Allegiance. Each week in 'morning business' in the Senate or 'morning hour' on Mondays and Tuesdays in the House (which, strangely, lasts for an hour and a half), time is also given over for members to give a five-minute speech on any topic they choose.

The debates determine the final fate of legislation. When a bill has been reported by a committee and placed on the calendar of the House or Senate it will be debated and subjected to attempts to amend it before a vote is taken on its final passage. For the vast majority of legislation, all that is needed is the approval of a simple majority of members voting in each chamber to pass into law.

House

Officially, it is the Speaker who chairs sessions in the House chamber, but apart from the most prestigious or politically important business, the duties are given to a more junior colleague to perform. Over the course of a normal day a number of Representatives will preside in place of the Speaker, calling the House to order, recognising members who wish to speak, ruling on points of order and overseeing voting procedures.

The structure of a debate on a bill on the House floor is determined by the rule (discussed in chapter 5). An example of a rule is given in Box 6.1. In this example the terms of debate are established for a bill concerning safety in transportation. It states that 'any time after the adoption of this resolution the Speaker may . . . declare the House resolved into the Committee of the Whole House on the state of the Union for consideration of the bill'. This is a procedural device to allow the debate to take place. Any meeting of the full House requires that half the total membership, some 218 members, be present before business can commence. This is known as a *quorum*. By resolving itself into the *Committee of the Whole*, the House can continue with its business with a quorum of only 100 members.

The rule then waives the first reading of the bill, another technical procedure which prevents the lengthy process of the whole bill being read aloud before debate can proceed. It decrees that the time set aside for debate will be evenly divided between the 'chairman and ranking minority member of the Committee on Transportation and Infrastructure'. This determines who will be managing the bill on the floor. The bill managers control the time available for debate and allocate it to members who wish to speak. The job is usually given to the chair and ranking member of the committee which reported the bill, who often work with the party leaders and whips to ensure the passage, defeat or alteration of the bill, depending on their preference.

Box 6.1   An example of a rule

107th Congress, 1st Session, H.RES.36

Providing for consideration of the bill (H.R. 554) to establish a program, coordinated by the National Transportation Safety Board, of assistance to families of passengers involved in rail passenger accidents.

Resolved, That at any time after the adoption of this resolution the Speaker may, pursuant to clause 2(b) of rule XVIII, declare the House resolved into the Committee of the Whole House on the state of the Union for consideration of the bill (H.R. 554) to establish a program, coordinated by the National Transportation Safety Board, of assistance to families of passengers involved in rail passenger accidents. The first reading of the bill shall be dispensed with. General debate shall be confined to the bill and shall not exceed one hour equally divided and controlled by the chairman and ranking minority member of the Committee on Transportation and Infrastructure. After general debate the bill shall be considered for amendment under the five-minute rule. Each section of the bill shall be considered as read. During consideration of the bill for amendment, the Chairman of the Committee of the Whole may accord priority in recognition on the basis of whether the Member offering an amendment has caused it to be printed in the portion of the Congressional Record designated for that purpose in clause 8 of rule XVIII. Amendments so printed shall be considered as read. At the conclusion of consideration of the bill for amendment the Committee shall rise and report the bill to the House with such amendments as may have been adopted. The previous question shall be considered as ordered on the bill and amendments thereto to final passage without intervening motion except one motion to recommit with or without instructions.

The rule also provides for the amendments under 'the five-minute rule'. The five-minute rule allows members to propose amendments and allocates five minutes for speeches in favour of each amendment and five minutes for speeches against. However, this time is regularly extended at members' requests.

Senate

Officially, the Vice-President of the United States is the presiding officer of the Senate. However, this role is usually only fulfilled on ceremonial occasions or when the Senate is tied on a vote and the Vice-President appears to cast the deciding ballot. In the absence of the Vice-President, the job of presiding officer falls to the *President pro tempore*, traditionally the longest serving member of the majority party. In practice, the President pro tempore will in turn delegate the duties of presiding over debates to other, more junior, members of the majority party.

Filibuster

The Senate as a whole is more accommodating to individual members' requests than the more formally disciplined House. Debates are often much slower and less focused than those in the House. One of the most important differences between debates in the two chambers is the possibility of a *filibuster* in the Senate. The Senate has no Rules Committee and instead determines the length and structure of its debates by unanimous consent agreements. Such agreements, however, can be disrupted by a single member. One such disruption is the filibuster. On occasions, a Senator opposed to a proposal (but aware that it is likely to be approved) will hold up proceedings by rising to speak on the Senate floor and once recognised by the presiding officer continuing to talk and talk and talk and talk. Once a Senator has the floor, he cannot be stopped from speaking unless he himself yields to another Senator. The idea behind the filibuster is to disrupt proceedings to such an extent that supporters of the proposal will attempt to negotiate a compromise or withdraw the measure entirely. As the Senator continues to talk, no other floor business can take place, forcing other scheduled debates down the calendar; a tactic which is particularly effective in the last days of the Congress. While the filibuster is taking place, proponents of the measure have to try to ensure that their fellow supporters remain close to the Senate floor. At any time, opponents may call for a quorum count and if too few Senators are present, the Senate will adjourn. Alternatively, on an issue where the Senate is closely divided, there is a danger of enough supporters of the measure leaving the Capitol that a vote could be called by the filibustering Senator and the measure may be defeated. These are particular dangers towards the end of the week when Senators are looking to return home to their constituencies. Faced with these problems, the proponents of the measure may choose to withdraw it for another time, or to negotiate.

The filibuster was immortalised in Frank Capra's excellent 1939 film *Mr Smith Goes to Washington*, where an honest but naive young Senator, Jefferson Smith (played by James Stewart) talks until he collapses to prevent the passage of a resolution expelling him from the Senate on false charges. The most famous instance in real life occurred in 1957 when South Carolina Senator Strom Thurmond spoke continuously for twenty-four hours and eighteen minutes to prevent the passage of civil rights legislation. Thurmond still holds the record for the longest filibuster. As long as they stay on their feet during a filibuster, Senators can speak on any subject they wish or, if they like, simply read from a text. Louisiana's legendary former Senator and Governor Huey P. Long was no stranger to the filibuster (once lasting fifteen hours), and would frequently spend the time reading from Shakespeare and cookery recipes for what he called 'pot-likkers'.

In order to prevent filibusters succeeding, the Senate rules were changed in 1917 to adopt the process of *cloture*. Today, if two-thirds of the Senate (currently sixty Senators) approve, a vote can close the debate, stopping the filibuster. Despite this, the filibuster is still an effective tool, largely because of the difficulty of achieving the two-thirds majority. Aside from the filibuster, Senate debates are traditionally more accommodating of individual members, and not so dominated by a few knowledgeable or experienced members as House debates can often be.

Amendments

In the Senate, any member can offer any amendment to any bill during the floor debate. They will have the opportunity to rise and propose their amendment, a short debate can take place and then the matter will be put to a vote. The process for offering and debating amendments in the House is the same, but members face restrictions as to the type of amendments which can be offered. Restrictions can be placed by the Rules Committee, who (if their decision is accepted by the House as a whole) can decree all or parts of a bill exempt from amendment. A permanent restriction faced by House members is that an amendment will be ruled out of order if, in the opinion of the Speaker, it is not *germane*, meaning that the amendment must concern the same issue as the bill it seeks to change. In the Senate, non-germane amendments are allowed and, as such, Senators can attempt to attach any provision to any bill, regardless of its relevance.

Purpose of amendments

While all amendments have the same goal – to change the content of the bill being debated – the motivation behind them can differ greatly. *Perfecting* amendments seek to correct or improve the legislation. These can be offered for a number of reasons: the supporters of the bill may wish to alter parts in order to reach a compromise which will attract more support in the final vote, members may attempt to attach riders to the bill to ensure their state or district benefits from the legislation, or it may be a genuine attempt to remedy a minor fault in the bill. *Wrecking* amendments are designed not to make the bill better, but to alter it to such an extent that would make its final passage unlikely. Opponents may offer an amendment which would make the legislation more radical, hoping that enough supporters of the bill will join opponents to vote for the provision, but that the amended bill will persuade wavering members to help defeat the final measure. During the passage of the 1964 Civil Rights Act, Congressman Howard Smith of Virginia, a staunch opponent of the legislation, offered an amendment extending the act to cover discrimination of women. Enough supporters of civil rights approved of this extension, that the amendment was adopted. Smith had hoped that the change would make the bill unpalatable to persuade enough members to join with the existing opponents to ensure its final defeat. The plan backfired however, and the Act along with Smith's amendment eventually passed into law. *Substitute* amendments seek to replace the bill in its entirety. Opponents will offer a complete alternative to the legislation, rather than attempting to form coalitions in support of a series of different amendments. Substitute amendments take a commitment of time and resources to write and will often come from the party hierarchy.

Voting

Once an amendment has been debated, or the amendment process has been completed and the bill is ready for a final decision, the presiding officer will call for a vote. The procedures differ slightly in the House and Senate.

Voting in the House

The first vote on an amendment or bill will be a voice-vote. The matter for decision will be announced and all those who support the measure will call 'aye' and all those who oppose it will call 'no'. The presiding officer will then announce which side has appeared to have won. Especially on uncontroversial issues, the opinion of the majority of the House will be obvious and the result will stand. On more closely contested decisions, a recorded vote may be requested at the behest of the necessary number of members (twenty-five in the Committee of the Whole). Through a system of lights and bells in the Capitol Building and surrounding offices, members will be alerted that a recorded vote is taking place, allowing them to make their way to the chamber. Once members arrive, they vote electronically. Each member has a credit-card sized voting card which they place in one of nearly forty voting machines located about the House chamber and press the appropriate button to vote 'yea', 'nay' or 'present'. Members are allowed to vote 'present' when they have no opinion on or knowledge of the issue or do not wish to express their opinion, but do not want their constituents to think they were simply absent. As members cast their vote it is registered against their name on a large electronic display above the Speaker's chair. Most votes last fifteen minutes to allow members to come from around the Capitol to vote, but this time limit can be extended at the discretion of the presiding officer. Once the time has elapsed the presiding officer announces the final result.

Voting in the Senate

There are occasions in the Senate when the process of voting itself is dispensed with. If the mood of the Senate on an issue is obvious, the presiding officer will suggest that 'without objection' the motion is accepted or rejected. If no one objects, the decision stands. Voice-votes and roll-call (recorded) votes are also used by the Senate. Unlike the House, there is no provision for electronic voting. When a recorded vote is called for, Senators gather in the chamber and a clerk calls their names one by one to which they respond with their vote. It is the smaller size of the Senate which makes this possible.

Recorded votes

Recorded votes are often called for practical reasons, because the House or Senate are evenly divided and the result cannot be precisely obtained by a voice-vote. It can, though, also be a political manoeuvre. Once a member has registered their opinion in a recorded vote, that information is in the public domain and can be viewed by voters or used by opponents in an election campaign. It is also accepted that members should attend a vote whenever physically possible. A poor attendance record in recorded votes can be used by opponents as evidence of a Senator or Representative not doing their job.

Consequently, calling for a recorded vote can be a tactic by supporters of a measure which they feel has public support to try and compel their colleagues to come to the chamber and publicly register their vote.

Do floor debates change anything?

In principle, debates encapsulate the essence of representative democracy. The Senators and Representatives chosen by the people, gather to consider legislative proposals and to persuade each other of the best course of action. When the arguments have been made and considered, a free vote decides the outcome. However doubts have been raised as to whether debates in Congress make any real difference.

Speaking in the 1930s, Senator Carter Glass said 'In the twenty-eight years that I have been a member of one or the other branches of Congress, I have never known a speech to change a vote'.[1] The accusation is that on any one issue, members' minds are made up long before legislation gets to a debate. This can be seen as a function of committee power (members deferring to the wishes of the specialist panel), constituency pressures (members determining the direction of their vote by a judgement as to the attitude of the majority of their voters) or following a party line. In such cases, it could be argued that such factors have more of an impact on the result of the vote than any argument put forward in a debate. Critics of the Congressional process could also point to the fact that in most cases only a small percentage of members who cast votes are actually present on the floor to hear the debate and as such could not have been affected by the arguments put forward there.

New York Congresswoman, Bella Abzug disagrees with this assessment. Writing in 1972 she argued

There is a theory around here . . . that to attend a debate on the floor is a waste of time. Since everybody has his mind made up in advance, the theory goes, what's the point of going to a debate? . . . Well that's the theory, and I, obviously, don't buy it. I hardly ever leave the Floor when the House is in session, because what I was sent here to do is sit and watch and participate. Besides, I don't think debate is a waste of time. I have seen my own arguments sway votes.[2]

Often speeches in debates are not aimed at persuading other members listening. They can be strategic tools designed to state a member's position for public consumption or to satisfy an interest group. Alternatively, coalition or party leaders can use the debate to indicate their support for a particular measure as a message to their supporters. However, in particularly close votes, the power of argument during a floor debate should not be dismissed. A powerful oration can be essential in persuading wavering opponents or convincing existing supporters to stand by their view.

House-Senate Conference

Once a bill has been debated, amended and succeeded in a final vote, that is not the end of the legislative process. One of the difficulties presented by a bicameral legislature is that once each chamber has considered the same legislation, with the addition of committee and floor amendments, two very different versions of a bill can emerge. In order for the legislation to be sent to the President for his signature, one single bill, agreed by both the House and Senate is needed. Where the differences are minor or uncontroversial, the process of reconciling the House and Senate is often straightforward. The chamber which first passed the legislation has an opportunity to consider the changes made by their opposite number and accept the new version of the bill. If they cannot accept the new version, a House-Senate Conference is called.

The House-Senate Conference committee meets on the Senate side of the Capitol Building. Membership of the conference is determined by the party leaders in the respective chambers, but will usually consists of members (and especially leaders) of the committee or subcommittee which originally considered the issue. These members will have the in-depth knowledge of the issue necessary to negotiate on behalf of the chamber. Shepsle and Weingast have argued that this process in itself increases committee power, by effectively providing its members with a veto over parts of legislation in conference.

The conference itself is a forum for discussion, negotiation and compromise. The two delegations are given the task of producing a single piece of legislation which will be acceptable to both the House and Senate. Sections of the bill can be amended or dropped entirely to facilitate agreement between the conferees. Each side of the conference is expected to defend their chamber's version of the legislation as far as possible, but ultimately they are free to choose on which issues to give way.

In the vast majority of cases, the conferees will reach a compromise agreeable to at least a majority of each delegation. Not all members of the conference will have gained all they wanted, but it is in their interests that a final bill emerge. Only on rare occasions will a conference fail to reach agreement, an eventuality which would doom the legislation at this late stage. Once the conference has finished its deliberations, the final version of the bill is sent back to the floors of the House and Senate for their approval. Attached to the bill will be a statement explaining the conference's decisions. If either the House or Senate does not approve of the changes made, they can vote to either recommit the legislation, sending it back to the conference for further consideration, or to reject the bill entirely. However, in practice, the majority conference reports are accepted by the both the House and Senate and the legislation is sent to the White House for the President's signature.

In itself, the decision to call a conference, rather than accept the other chamber's version, can be politically motivated and controversial. In February 2002, campaign finance reform legislation was up for debate on the House floor having successfully passed the Senate some months before. The Republican House leadership opposed the legislation, but were aware that it was likely that enough Republicans would join with the Democrats to pass the bill. One tactic opponents of the legislation used was to offer multiple amendments in an attempt to make the House's version of the bill sufficiently different from the Senate. They hoped that if they succeeded, the Senate would be reluctant to accept the House's alterations and a House-Senate conference would be called. With the majority party leadership able to influence which House members would be sent to the conference, there was a serious threat that the bill would not survive a conference or that it would be significantly altered. The attempt was unsuccessful, however, as with only minor differences between the two versions, the Senate accepted the House bill with no need for a conference.

Summary

If a bill is to become a law, it must gain the approval of both the House and Senate in a floor debate. For most legislation, a simple majority is required. The procedures for debating and voting are similar in the House and Senate, although the rules of the Senate afford individual members more scope to disrupt proceedings. The floor debate also gives members an opportunity to offer amendments to legislation. The motivation behind such amendments can vary. If different versions of the same bill emerge from the House and Senate, it is often necessary to call a House-Senate Conference to iron out the differences before the bill can be sent to the White House for the President's signature.

Notes

1 P. F. Boller Jr., *Congressional Anecdotes* (Oxford: Oxford University Press, 1991), p. 181.
2 Ibid.

President and Congress

President John Tyler stated that he enjoyed good health, and felt much better since Congress had finally adjourned. (L. A. Godbright, 1869)

At the heart of the Constitution is the separation of power between the President of the United States and Congress. The President has the roles of chief diplomat, Commander-in-Chief of the Armed Forces and, as head of the executive branch, the responsibility for executing the laws passed by Congress. While the President and Congress were given separate powers and responsibilities, the Founding Fathers also ensured that each would be checked by the other.

Checks and balances

The President has the power to appoint ambassadors, federal court judges, Supreme Court justices, cabinet members and other top federal posts. Each of these appointments, however, must be confirmed by a vote in the Senate. The Constitution gives the President the power to sign treaties on behalf of the United States, but these must also pass the approval of the Senate (requiring a two-thirds majority). The actions of the departments and agencies of the executive branch are subject to scrutiny by Congressional committees who may, in exceptional circumstances, censure officers for their behaviour.

Members of Congress take the role of watchdog seriously. Committees spend a great deal of time questioning and scrutinising the departments and agencies who deal with the policies under the committees' jurisdiction. Many committees also maintain constant, more informal, communications with the agencies and their staff to keep informed as to the successes and failures of existing laws. The exact approach to the oversight role will vary between committees. One criticism of Congress is that too many committees approach oversight with a 'fire-fighter' approach, responding when a problem with the executive branch comes to light, rather than maintaining a more systematic style of surveillance.

When major problems arise, Congressional committees take centre stage in the investigation of what went wrong. Most of the time, such investigations are of little interest to anyone outside of the Washington establishment. Despite this, they can have a real effect. In 1983, the controversial head of the Environmental Protection Agency, Anne Gorsuch, was censured by the House of Representatives for obstructing Congressional oversight by refusing to supply certain documents. Following the censure, Gorsuch resigned. However, when Congress investigates the activities of the President and his key advisers, the process of oversight can capture the attention of the whole nation. In 1986, evidence began to emerge that the Reagan Administration had been covertly selling arms to Iran in exchange for the release of hostages held in Lebanon and then, in direct contravention of the law, passing on the profits of the sales to the 'Contra' rebels fighting in Nicaragua. A series of Congressional investigations discovered not only that had profits from the Iranian arm sales been diverted to the Nicaraguan rebels, but that members of the administration had lied to Congress in an attempt at a cover-up and had tried to subvert the process of Congressional oversight. While the President was never directly implicated himself, it did great damage to the remaining years of his Presidency.

Foreign policy

Most of this book has been concerned with domestic policy; the area in which Congress is usually dominant. Foreign policy, on the other hand, has been historically the domain of the President. Military action often needs immediate decisions, something which a Congress of 535 members is not best suited to take. However, as the example above shows, Congress also has a role to play.

The President is Commander-in-Chief of the Armed Forces and along with the Pentagon and State Department decides on America's military and diplomatic strategies. Like all power in Washington DC, the Constitution ensures that checks and balances exist. The Founding Fathers gave Congress the power to control the funding of the armed forces, to decide when war is declared and, in the case of the Senate, final approval over the appointment of ambassadors. Some of these powers have proven to be limited. Although it is Congress not the President which can officially declare war, the whole notion of declaring war has become outdated. Among others, the Vietnam, Gulf and Afghanistan Wars, were never officially declared. Indeed, despite being involved in numerous conflicts, the United States has not declared war on a nation since World War II. Similarly, while Congress has the power to withdraw funds from any military action it disapproves of, the public support of the armed forces which generally greets military action makes Congress wary of being seen to oppose the President. One main criticism of Congress during the Vietnam War was that it shirked its responsibilities by, in the Gulf of Tonkin resolution, giving President Johnson a blank cheque to pursue the war in any way he wished.

However, these limitations do not mean that Congress is impotent in matters of foreign policy. When the Vietnam War started to lose popularity at home, it was Congress which began to reassert itself by limiting the funds available to President Nixon, in an attempt to control his policy. Determined to not repeat the mistakes of the past, Congress passed the War Powers Act in 1973. This Act formalised the role of Congress in checking the President's actions by controlling the funds for military action. Under the War Powers Act, the President on sending troops abroad must, within sixty days, gain formal approval from Congress. If such approval is not forthcoming, he has a further thirty days to withdraw the troops.

The War Powers Act, however, has been criticised for being ineffective. Critics argue that in the modern era many military actions are finished within ninety days, making the approval of Congress irrelevant. Furthermore, in the early stages of a conflict, Congress will be less willing to oppose military action with public support, making the President's task of gaining official sanction straightforward. Indeed, the War Powers Act would have been unlikely to make much difference to the Vietnam War which only began to lose American public support years after troops had been sent into action.

Congress can play a more effective role when foreign policy is not militarily based. Increasingly, economics, trade and actions through the United Nations and NATO are becoming as important as troops and bombs. Congress through its Armed Services and Foreign Affairs Committees can begin to have a real impact on policy. The Helms-Burton Act, passed in 1996, imposed stringent economic trade sanctions on the island of Cuba in attempt to isolate the Castro Government. This foreign policy initiative came not from the White House, but from Congress.

Impeachment

In the most extreme of circumstances, the Constitution gives Congress the power to remove the President from office through the process of *impeachment*.

On 19 December 1998 President William Jefferson Clinton became only the second President in the history of the United States to be impeached by the House of Representatives. The House voted to impeach on two articles, perjury before the Grand Jury and obstruction of justice, both relating to the President's affair with White House intern Monica Lewinsky and his subsequent denials. They rejected two other charges of perjury in another testimony and abuse of power. In line with the procedures laid out in the Constitution, the Senate then convened to try the President on the impeachment charges. If President Clinton was found guilty by the Senate he would have been the first President to be removed from office by the United States Congress. The trial was presided over by Supreme Court Chief Justice William H. Rhenquist and all 100 Senators were sworn in as the jury. It lasted until 12 February 1999, when the Senate voted to acquit the President of both charges. The Constitution requires a two-thirds majority to reach a guilty verdict, the charge of perjury was rejected with 45 Senators voting guilty, 55 voting to acquit; the charge of obstructing of justice saw the Senate tied 50–50, short of the 66 members needed to convict.

The Constitution states that the President may be removed from office through the process of impeachment by the House and conviction by the Senate if he has committed 'high crimes and misdemeanours'. This phrase is open to interpretation and central to the debate surrounding the Clinton impeachment was whether the President's actions could be classed as such. The first President to be impeached by the House was Andrew Johnson in 1868. He survived in office when the Senate fell short of the required two-thirds majority by a single vote. Officially, Johnson's misdemeanour was the sacking of an official in contravention of the then Tenure of Office Act. However, in reality the charges against Johnson were a pretence for a wider political dispute over the role of government in the post-Civil War period of reconstruction. In Johnson's case, the impeachment process was used as a political tool in a battle between President and Congress.

The same allegation was made by the Clinton White House: that the charges against the President were nothing to do with any crime Clinton may have committed but were a partisan attempt by Republicans to damage the President. Hillary Clinton went so far as to describe the charges as part of a 'vast right-wing conspiracy'. Supporters of the President pointed to the fact that the charges were based on a report from independent council Kenneth Starr. Starr had been appointed in 1994 to investigate allegations against the Clintons involving a failed land development deal in Arkansas known as 'Whitewater'. Having failed to find damning evidence in that case, Starr was given permission to widen his enquiries. After examining issues such as the suicide of White House counsel Vince Foster, the firing of staff in the White

House travel office and invasion of privacy using FBI files, Starr finally found evidence that President Clinton had lied about having sexual relations with Monica Lewinsky. Clinton first denied the affair completely, declaring 'I did not have sexual relations with that woman', but as the evidence mounted he was forced to admit to wrongdoing.

The argument over impeachment centred around the severity of his misdemeanour. Defenders of the President argued that Starr's report was partisan and essentially about Clinton's private life, which did not fall into the category of 'high crimes and misdemeanours'. They pointed to the lurid details included in the report, arguing that they were unnecessary and an attempt to undermine the President. Supporters of impeachment countered that the charges were based on evidence of perjury and obstruction of justice which contradicted the oath the President had taken on assuming office to 'faithfully execute the office of the President of the United States . . . and preserve, protect and defend the constitution of the United States'.

As the impeachment process began, it became clear that this would be a largely partisan battle. With some notable exceptions, Republicans were arguing for impeachment and Democrats taking a position against. Such an alignment would give advocates of impeachment enough votes for victory in the House, but would fall short of the two-thirds majority needed in the Senate. Ultimately, it can be argued that Bill Clinton was saved from the ignominy of becoming the first President to be removed from office by the power of public opinion. As the debate on impeachment proceeded, opinion polls showed a marked rise in support for the President. While the majority of people disapproved of the President's behaviour, there was a clear feeling that the public did not want to see him removed from office and approved of the job he was doing as President. Rather than the impeachment process harming his public standing, Clinton's approval ratings continued to rise to a high of 70 per cent in February 1999.

Legislative leadership

The Constitution states that the President of the United States 'shall from time to time give to the Congress Information of the State of the Union, and recommend to their Consideration such Measures as he shall judge necessary and expedient'. The Founding Fathers obviously saw some role for the President in initiating legislation, but in an advisory role. In the early years of the Republic, Congress jealously guarded its position as the sole legislative authority. The President had primacy in affairs of defence and foreign policy, but his role in the legislative process was largely restricted to the power of the veto. Attempts were made by various Presidents to play a larger role in domestic legislation (most notably the 'progressive Presidents' Theodore Roosevelt (1901–9) and Woodrow Wilson (1913–21)), but any advances in the power of the President remained minimal.

The situation changed dramatically with the election of Democrat Franklin D. Roosevelt in 1932. America was suffering from the Great Depression, unemployment reached unprecedented levels and the banking system was in danger of collapse. With no national system of welfare and the states unable to cope, poverty became widespread. President Roosevelt was elected on a promise of using the federal government to address these problems. His 'New Deal' programme, which for the first time established a national welfare system, transformed the role of the federal government by involving it in areas previously accepted as the domain of state government. Roosevelt also transformed the power of the presidency. For the first time, the President took the lead in formulating legislation. The first 100 days of the Franklin Roosevelt Presidency witnessed a whirlwind of legislative activity with a raft of legislative proposals produced by the White House and adopted by the Democrat-dominated Congress. Critics charged that during this period Congress failed in its Constitutional responsibilities; rather than act as a deliberative legislative assembly, it became little more than a rubber stamp for the President's programme.

This period of presidential legislative leadership was unprecedented in American history and was never to be repeated again. However, the New Deal set a precedent that allowed future administrations to play a much greater role in the formulation of legislation. All presidential candidates now run for election promising changes in domestic policy, whether it be healthcare, education, welfare or the environment, even though Congress remains the only body which can introduce legislation and pass laws.

The power of the President to get the legislation he desires remains, in the words of Richard Neustadt, the 'power to persuade'. The President has no formal sanctions to compel Congress to consider and pass legislation he supports. Instead he must negotiate, bully and bribe (legally) members of Congress to persuade them to follow his wishes. The White House will work with party and committee leaders in Congress as well as individual members to try and achieve their legislative goals. Common inducements offered to members to persuade them to support the President will often involve a promise of future support for that member's pet project, or to ensure that their home state or district will benefit from legislative proposals on other matters.

At the other end of the spectrum, the White House will often attempt to punish members who do not respond to White House pressures. This approach can backfire. In 2001, when Republican Senator Jim Jeffords voted against key provisions of President George W. Bush's economic package he found himself shunned by the White House. He was not invited to the annual 'teacher of the year' award at the White House, despite the fact that education was one of his main interests in the Senate and that the recipient of the award came from his home state of Vermont. The attitude of the Bush Administration towards Jeffords was reportedly influential in finally persuading him to leave the Republican Party, a development which gave the Democrats control of the Senate.

The White House will try and use the knowledge and expertise supplied by its agencies and departments to persuade members to support the administration's policy. However, much will often depend on the ability of the President or his Congressional liaison staff to personally persuade members to give them their support. President Lyndon B. Johnson, who was famous for his persuasive skills while Senate Majority Leader, attempted to use the same techniques from the White House (see Appendix 7.1). President Jimmy Carter had a great deal of difficulty in his relations with Congress, which has been frequently attributed to his inexperience and that of his aides in Washington politics. Carter had previously held office as Governor of Georgia. In contrast President Ronald Reagan, who like Carter only had political experience outside of Washington, benefited from appointing experienced former members of Congress and Capitol Hill staffers to his liaison team. They managed to use their contacts to develop relationships and work with Congress with some success.

The President's ability to persuade is inevitably affected by his popularity in the country as a whole. A President with strong public backing for his proposals will be in an advantageous position when attempting to persuade members to lend their support. Nothing focuses the mind of Representatives and Senators more than the prospect of their decisions affecting the level of public support they hold in their district or state. Consequently, in the immediate aftermath of an election victory, a new President is expected to have a 'honeymoon period' when they can use the political capital gained by their election to begin to persuade Congress to pass their election platform into law.

This notion of 'political capital' is central to the power to persuade. The goodwill a new President brings to the position must be used judiciously and can easily be squandered. Two contrasting examples of the use of political capital are the first few months of the presidencies of Bill Clinton and Ronald Reagan. In fairness to Clinton, he arrived at the White House with a less certain mandate from the voters than many of his predecessors. A strong showing by third-party candidate H. Ross Perot ensured that Clinton was elected to the presidency with less than 50 per cent of the popular vote. Nevertheless, any political kudos that Clinton entered the White House with soon diminished following a series of public relations disasters which damaged his public standing. One of the Clinton Administration's first acts was to announce an end to the ban on gay men and women serving in the armed forces. However, the President soon discovered the limitations of Washington politics when he ran into staunch opposition from the military and was forced to compromise on a 'don't ask, don't tell' policy which satisfied no one. Soon after, in May of 1993 a scandal erupted when seven workers in the White House travel office were abruptly fired, leading to accusations of abuse of power which triggered a Congressional enquiry. In the same month, President Clinton received a, now infamous, $200 haircut aboard Air Force One while it sat on a runway at Los Angeles Airport, causing other flights to be delayed. The negative impact on the popularity of the new administration did nothing to help the difficulties President Clinton faced in persuading Congress to pass his legislative agenda.

Clinton's biggest difficulty in providing legislative leadership came with his proposals on extending the scope of federal healthcare. The issue had formed a central plank in his election manifesto, and on arrival in the White House the President placed his wife (now Senator) Hillary Rodham Clinton in charge of a commission to research and formulate the plan. The plan was an important part of the Administration's legislative agenda. Their proposals were presented to Congress in early 1994, but despite Clinton's own party, the Democrats, having a majority in both the House and Senate, the plan died in Congress. The Administration blamed interest groups, specifically medical insurance firms who would lose customers if federal healthcare entitlement was expanded, for pressuring members of Congress to abandon the scheme. There was some truth in this as insurance groups did spend a great deal of money opposing the plan. The Health Insurance Association of America ran a series of television adverts which depicted two average middle-aged Americans 'Harry' and 'Louise' examining Clinton's proposals while discussing its 'hidden costs' and the loss of 'provider choice'. However, the Administration's inexperience in dealing with

Congress was also a major factor. There was criticism of Hillary Clinton's task force which met behind closed doors before producing a fully formed programme. The scheme itself was said to be complicated and difficult for the average American to understand, let alone support. The lesson to be learned by the Administration was that while the White House can produce and support legislative programmes, Congress holds the sole power to bring such schemes into law. The White House must work *with* Congress rather than dictate *to* it.

In contrast, in 1981, the new Reagan Administration used his honeymoon period to its full. The United States was suffering from an economic downturn and Reagan had come to office pledging to reduce the size of government and revitalise the economy. His budget proposed cuts in taxes and most areas of spending (although defence spending was to rise) and the elimination of many federal regulations on businesses. The proposals faced fierce opposition in Congress; members were aware that many of the programmes which faced cuts benefited their constituents. Interest groups also campaigned against cuts in programmes they supported. With such opposition, it looked highly unlikely that President Reagan would succeed in passing much of his budget through Congress. During his Presidency, Reagan became known as the 'Great Communicator' and he used his communication skills to appeal directly to the voters. This strategy, known as 'going public', is often a last resort, but when used successfully can be a potent weapon. He appealed to the public to contact their Senators and Representatives in support of his economic plan and the appeal worked. Faced with a barrage of letters from their voters, Congress relented and passed many of Reagan's key proposals. Speaking to the nation later that year, Reagan thanked the public for their support

> All the lobbying, the organized demonstrations, and the cries of protest by those whose way of life depends on maintaining government's wasteful ways were no match for your voices, which were heard loud and clear in these marble halls of government. And you made history with your telegrams, your letters, your phone calls and, yes, personal visits to talk to your elected representatives . . . Because of what you did, Republicans and Democrats in the Congress came together and passed the most sweeping cutbacks in the history of the Federal budget.[1]

Veto

If the position of the President is limited in terms of initiating legislation, the Constitution gives a clear role at the other end of the legislative process. Once a bill has passed both the House and Senate, it is sent to the President for his signature. On receipt of the legislation he has three options:

- Sign the bill – passing it into law.
- Do nothing – where, after ten days, it will pass into law without his signature.
- Veto the bill, sending it back to Congress.

If the legislation is vetoed, Congress can pass it into law over the objections of the President if a two-thirds majority is obtained in both the House and Senate. Historically, this has been difficult to achieve with less than 5 per cent of all vetoes being overridden by Congress (see Table 7.1).

The use of the veto should not be viewed as a decision taken in isolation. Throughout the whole legislative process, the White House will be talking with Congressional leaders and the objections of the President will be known before a bill

Table 7.1 Presidential vetoes (1789–2001)

President	Regular vetoes	Pocket vetoes*	Total vetoes	Vetoes overridden
George Washington	2	—	2	—
John Adams	—	—	—	—
Thomas Jefferson	—	—	—	—
James Madison	5	2	7	—
James Monroe	1	—	1	—
John Quincy Adams	—	—	—	—
Andrew Jackson	5	7	12	—
Martin Van Buren	—	1	1	—
William Harrison	—	—	—	—
John Tyler	6	4	10	1
James K. Polk	2	1	3	—
Zachary Taylor	—	—	—	—
Millard Fillmore	—	—	—	—
Franklin Pierce	9	—	9	5
James Buchanan	4	3	7	—
Abraham Lincoln	2	5	7	—
Andrew Johnson	21	8	29	15
Ulysses S. Grant	45	48	93	4
Rutherford B. Hayes	12	1	13	1
James A. Garfield	—	—	—	—
Chester A. Arthur	4	8	12	1
Grover Cleveland	304	110	414	2
Benjamin Harrison	19	25	44	1
Grover Cleveland	42	128	170	5
William McKinley	6	36	42	—
Theodore Roosevelt	42	40	82	1
William H. Taft	30	9	39	1
Woodrow Wilson	33	11	44	6
Warren G. Harding	5	1	6	—
Calvin Coolidge	20	30	50	4
Herbert C. Hoover	21	16	37	3
Franklin D. Roosevelt	372	263	635	9
Harry S. Truman	180	70	250	12

Table 7.1 continued

President	Regular vetoes	Pocket vetoes*	Total vetoes	Vetoes overridden
Dwight D. Eisenhower	73	108	181	2
John F. Kennedy	12	9	21	—
Lyndon B. Johnson	16	14	30	—
Richard M. Nixon	26	17	43	7
Gerald R. Ford	48	18	66	12
James Earl Carter	13	18	31	2
Ronald Reagan	39	39	78	9
George Bush	29	15	44	1
William J. Clinton	37	1	38	2
George W. Bush	—	—	—	—
Total	1484	1066	2551	106

Pocket vetoes are those used when Congress has adjourned and, as such, cannot be overridden.

reaches his desk. A threat of a veto is one of the tools the White House can use to try to persuade Congress to shape legislation in line with the President's agenda. In 1994, when Congress was debating Bill Clinton's healthcare proposals, the President, afraid that his plan would be watered down, warned Congress 'If you send me legislation that does not guarantee every American private health insurance that can never be taken away, you will force me to take this pen, veto the legislation, and we'll come back here and start all over again'. Such an inflexible approach can backfire as Clinton found when no healthcare bill was reported at all.

Using the veto can be a risky strategy. As an essentially negative tool, by blocking the proposals of Congress the President can appear to be siding with inaction over action. He also faces the possibility of an embarrassing defeat if the veto is overridden. Alternatively, opponents of the President in Congress may attempt to force a confrontation with the White House over a veto in the hope of winning the support of the public, especially during an election year. However, as Newt Gingrich discovered in 1995, this strategy can backfire.

The confrontation between the Republican leadership and President Clinton took place over the budget. As is customary, the President had submitted his budget to Congress for consideration at the beginning of the year. There was little prospect of the Republican-dominated Congress accepting Clinton's proposals. The Republicans wanted to see large cuts in federal spending to balance the budget which had been in deficit for many years. The White House was willing to accept some cuts, but objected to the level of reductions in the Republican plans. Such a situation where the White House and Congress disagree on the plans for the budget is not unusual, indeed it is quite common. Normally, to ensure that the Government is funded while the negotiations over the budget are continuing, Congress will pass a *continuing reso-lution* to keep programmes afloat until a compromise has been reached. In 1995, however, the Republican Party leader-ship in Congress ensured that the continuing resolution con-tained some of the budget cuts that Clinton was opposed to. Since their landslide victory in 1994, the President had been on the back foot and House Speaker Newt Gingrich was looking to push home his advantage. Accordingly, the con-tinuing resolution passed by Congress contained some of the budget cuts for healthcare wanted by the Republican Congress. President Clinton vetoed the measure and, on 14 November 1995, because there was no budget to fund the machinery, the Government partially shutdown. Almost half of the federal employees were sent home from work, national monuments and parks closed and new applications for welfare payments could not be processed.

This showdown between the President and Congress was a dangerous play by both sides. The Republican leadership hoped the blame would lie with the White House for blocking their attempts to balance the budget, a goal which seemed to have support in the country. The President argued that he was protecting vital public services from attack by the Republican Party. In his address to the nation announcing the shutdown he laid out his case,

> Today, as of noon, almost half of the federal government employees are idle. The government is partially shutting down because Congress has failed to pass the straightforward legislation necessary to keep the government running without imposing sharp hikes in Medicare premiums and deep cuts in education and the environment . . . Let me be clear – we must balance the budget. I proposed to Congress a balanced budget, but Congress refused to enact it. Congress has even refused to give me the line-item veto to help me achieve further deficit reduction. But we must balance this budget without resorting to their priorities, without their unwise cuts in Medicare and Medicaid, in education and the environment . . . it is my solemn responsibility to stand against a budget plan that is bad for America and to stand up for a balanced budget that is good for America. And that is exactly what I intend to do.[2]

The deadlock lasted until 27 January 1996 with the Government shutting down twice during that period.

In this instance, it was the President's actions which won public support. As the deadlock over the budget continued, opinion polls showed support for the President's position. On 15 November, the second day of the shutdown, 49 per cent of those questioned said they blamed the Republican leadership for the crisis, with only 26 per cent blaming Bill Clinton. The President's pitch to the nation seemed to have worked, and he maintained this lead in the opinion polls throughout the deadlock. By 10 January, 57 per cent of voters supported the President, with 36 per cent backing the Republican leadership's stand.[3] Ultimately, a compromise was reached between the two sides, but one that was viewed more as a victory for Clinton than for the Republicans. The Republican Chairman of the House Budget Committee admitted 'We did the wrong strategy. That's okay. We tried. It didn't work. Now we've got to be smarter'.[4]

In this case President Clinton's use of the veto was a masterstroke. By painting himself as the guardian of public services, he galvanised public support in a way which he had failed to do during the previous three years. With the economy strong and support for the President rising in the opinion polls he proceeded to defeat the Senate Majority Leader Republican Bob Dole in the 1996 election.

Divided government

The case of the Government shutdown illustrates how conflict can occur when Congress and the presidency are controlled by different parties. Such *divided government* has been a regular situation in the United States in recent years. In the period 1933–69, the same party controlled both branches of government for all but eight years. Since 1969 however, divided government has become the norm, and in that time the President has faced a Congress with either one or both chambers controlled by the opposing party for all but six years.

Explanations of why divided government has become so

frequent vary. During the 1980s it was often argued that the parties' reputations meant that voters preferred Republicans to run the White House and Democrats to run Congress; Republicans were seen as stronger on foreign policy (especially in the Cold War terms of being anti-Communist), whereas the Democrats were identified with better social welfare. Consequently, the argument ran, the electors were simply electing the parties to the branch of government which best suited their policies. However, this explanation faced difficulties in the 1990s when between 1995 and 2001 the electorate kept a Democrat in the White House and a Republican majority in Congress. An alternative explanation is that voters engage in 'split-ticket voting' in a deliberate attempt to ensure that one party does not become all powerful. This is often attributed to a general dissatisfaction with both political parties.[5]

It would be logical to assume that the White House and Congress would be able to co-operate more easily when they are controlled by the same party. Indeed, there is evidence that when one party controls both branches of government, the President is more successful in passing his proposals and less likely to use the veto than under divided government.[6] However, the difference should not be overstated. As Bill Clinton found with his healthcare plan, unified government is no guarantor of Presidential success. Indeed, David Mayhew has gone so far as to argue that 'it does not seem to make all that much difference whether party control of the American Government happens to be unified or divided'.[7]

Summary

The Constitution of the United States ensures that each power given to the President or Congress is checked by the other branch of government. Since 1933, domestic policy has been characterised by co-operation and competition between the White House and Congress. Despite this, Congress remains the only body which can pass federal laws. Congress acts as a watchdog over the executive branch, with the ultimate power to remove the President if he is found guilty of 'high crimes and misdemeanours'. In turn, the President has the ability to veto legislation passed by Congress, although if two-thirds of the House and Senate agree, the veto can be overturned. Foreign policy is usually the domain of the White House, but Congress has proved able to play a role in this area also.

Appendix: the Johnson treatment

On 23 January, 1964 the Senate Finance Committee was giving final consideration to a tax cut bill backed by President Johnson. On that morning, Senator Everett Dirksen surprised the White House by proposing an amendment which would repeal taxes on a wide range of luxury goods. The committee passed the amendment. The new cuts, it was estimated, would cost the treasury over $400 million, and threatened to endanger the success of both the bill and Johnson's budget. The president needed the committee to reconsider the amendment and reject it. Johnson took over the campaign to persuade committee members himself. While he trod carefully with senior committee members, he was not afraid to try and strong-arm others. What follows is a transcript of a telephone conversation between President Johnson and fellow Democrat and committee member Senator Abraham Ribicoff, who had supported and con-tributed to Dirksen's amendment.

Johnson: Hey Abe. Can't you go with us on this excise thing and let us get a bill? Goddamn it, you need to vote with me once in a while – just one time.

Ribicoff: Mr President, look. I made a commitment. President . . .

Let me say this – the Treasury Department is reaping the whirl-wind.

Johnson: I know it. I know it. We were ready to report this bill, and now we've got it just good and screwed up, and the Democrats are going to be a miserable failure in the eyes of the country. Now why can't you all meet at two o'clock, ad let's leave this excise like we had it before you met this morning?

Ribicoff: Well, I don't know how you're going to keep it – the thing was overwhelming.

Johnson: No, it's not. No. Clint Anderson is going to help us. Hartke will help us. And if you'll help us, we'll have it over. And I'll appreciate it and I'll remember it. Help me one way or the other.

Ribicoff: You know, just one word, Mr President –

Johnson: You've had these problems, executive, and you know we've had that damn bill there since September. And *every* day it's costing us $30 million in consumer income, every single day.

Ribicoff: One of my problems is one of the amendments in there is something in my home state that's already been announced.

Johnson: I know it, but every one of them has got it in there, my friend. But God almighty, I think about the problems I've had. And when you wanted to go on that committee, I just stood up and said, 'By God, it's going to be.'

Now, I just want one vote, and I want to get that bill out of there, and I've got to have it, Abe. And you've had problems. You've been an executive. And you can find a way to help me.

They've asked me to call you 40 times this year and I've never done it. But this time, when it means $400 or $500 million – this is going to be a whole motion to leave all the excises as they were before Williams and them got mad on the oil thing. And don't let John Williams and Everett Dirksen screw me this way.

Ribicoff: Let me see how I can save my face. I've got a problem –

Johnson: Don't you worry about saving your face. Your face is in damn good shape, and it's going to be better when I get with you. I'll save your face. [Ribicoff chuckles.] You save my face this afternoon, and I'll save your face tomorrow.

Ribicoff: Well some time, I would really like to talk to you.

Johnson: You can do it any hour, any hour. I've had 56 days in this job, and they've been the most miserable 56 I've ever had.

Ribicoff: You're doing good, sir.

Johnson: And my people are going [in] opposite directions. And now damn Harry Byrd goes one way and he says cut your damn budget, and I'll help you get your bill out. He called me yesterday and said it would be reported tomorrow. I thought it was all settled.

Ribicoff: You're doing great, Mr President. Honest to God. You're doing so great it isn't even –

Johnson: Will you go in there and help me this afternoon?

Ribicoff: Let me try. Let me see how I can work it out.

Johnson: You just work it out. Now don't say how. I don't give a damn about the details. I just want you to work it out. Will you?

Ribicoff: I'll do my – OK, Mr President.

Johnson: Bye.

Ribicoff: Bye.

Later that day the Senate Finance Committee voted 9 to 8 to reject the Dirksen amendment. The tax cut bill was reported by 12 to 5.

Source: Presidential Recordings Project, Miller Center.

Notes

1 R. Reagan, *Address to the Nation on Federal Tax Reduction Legislation, July 27, 1981*, Public Papers of the President.

2 William J. Clinton, *Address to the Nation, November 14, 1995*, Public Papers of the President.

3 Washington Post-ABC News poll, 10 Jan 1996.

4 CNN.com, *Third federal shutdown averted*, 27 January 1996.

5 M. Fiorina, *Divided Government* (Boston Allyn & Bacon, 1996), ch 4.

6 S. S. Smith, *The American Congress* (Boston: Houghton Mifflin, 1999), ch 3.

7 D. R. Mayhew, *Divided We Govern: Party Control, Lawmaking and Investigations, 1946–1990* (New Haven: Yale University Press, 1991), p. 198.

8

Congress, the media and interest groups

Any dictator would admire the uniformity and obedience of the U.S. media. (Noam Chomsky)

In the previous chapters, the relationship between the voters, parties, the President and members of Congress have been examined. This section looks at two other actors who impact on Congress: the media and interest groups.

Media

The media performs a crucial role in the American political process. The majority of voters will have little or no personal contact with Congress or its members. These voters rely heavily on newspapers, radio, television and the Internet for information about their elected representatives. This position gives the media the potential to influence the political agenda of the nation greatly. It also has opened up the media to accusations that it is not living up to its responsibilities.

Development of the modern media

In a country the size of the United States, the media has always had an important role to play in relaying information about the federal government to citizens across the nation. From the beginning of the republic until the twentieth century this role was the sole preserve of newspapers.

Newspapers in the United States are generally local concerns. In the early years of America this was a matter of practicality; the technology to distribute a daily newspaper across the whole nation was not available. Today, while one major national newspaper, *USA Today*, exists, locally produced broadsheets are still the norm. The most influential of newspapers, the *New York Times* and the *Washington Post* are still locally based.

As the twentieth century progressed, radio and television began to challenge the dominance of the printed word. These new mediums could respond quicker than newspapers and were often seen as being more politically neutral. Especially in the eighteenth century, newspapers were often openly partisan. The political establishment was quick to adapt to the development of the new media. President Franklin D. Roosevelt used radio to deliver his 'fireside chats' to the American public. John F. Kennedy, the first 'television President' used his good looks and easy manner to deliver his messages directly into the homes of the people. Still today, the President will deliver a weekly radio address on any subject of his choice and will on important occasions address the nation via television.

Newspapers still have an important role to play. They have retained the ability to pursue stories over a longer period of time and to undertake in-depth investigations, free from the pressures suffered by television and radio to report news on an hourly basis. The most famous of these investigations was the Watergate affair which, ultimately, led to the resignation of President Richard Nixon. The central figures behind revealing the scandal and the cover-up which followed were two reporters from the *Washington Post,* Carl Bernstein and Bob Woodward. Their efforts led to the award of a Pulitzer Prize and were immortalised in the film *All the President's Men* starring Robert Redford and Dustin Hoffman.

Entertainment v. information

The main criticism which has been levelled at the media is that there exists a conflict between providing entertainment and providing serious news, and that this conflict has led to the media, especially television, trivialising politics. Television is now the main source of news for the vast majority of the American public. Television companies are businesses which rely on advertising revenue to make a profit. In order to attract and retain advertisers, stations must keep people watching their shows. The need to entertain has become paramount.

It has been argued that the pressure to attract viewers has had two effects on television coverage of politics. The first effect is to shorten the amount of time spent on news stories. To avoid any danger of boring the audience into switching channels, news programmes have become fast moving, favouring short news items rather than detailed investigations and reliant on 'soundbites' over more in-depth interviews. Even the most complex of issues must be condensed into a few minutes to ensure the continued attention of the audience. The average length of a soundbite on American television during presidential election campaigns has shrunk from 43.1 seconds in 1968 to 8.2 seconds in 1996.[1] Noam Chomsky, a critic of media coverage of politics, quotes a source from ABC's *Nightline* (one of the more serious and respected news programmes), who described the ideal guest on the programme as someone who can restrict their answers to 30 seconds or less. It is easy to argue that such limitations make it impossible to investigate or explain complex political issues without gross oversimplification.

The second effect of the conflict between entertainment and news is the trivialising of political coverage. Television has been accused of focusing on sensational, salacious or trivial stories under the guise of news reports which reduce politics to a series of scandals, gaffes and personality issues. In 2001, Congressman Gary Condit of California found himself in the glare of the media spotlight. Condit, a conservative Democrat, was widely considered to be a rising star in Washington DC politics. He was willing to work with both Republicans and Democrats and with the House of Representatives closely divided between Democrats and Republicans following the 2000 election, members such as Condit became crucial in the battle for votes. It was no surprise when he was invited to join the Democrat leadership council. For all of Condit's political achievements and his growing importance in Congress, few outside of California's 18th district would probably have heard of Gary Condit. On 30 April 2001 Chandra Levy, who had been working for Congressman Condit as an intern, disappeared. As fears grew for her safety, it became known that Levy had been having an affair with the Congressman. Condit was far from open about his relationship with Chandra Levy and was accused by the police of being obstructive to their investigation. Police investigators removed items from his home and soon rumours circulated regarding any role Condit might have had in Levy's disappearance. Despite police statements insisting that Condit was not being investigated in any way in relation to Levy's actual disappearance, the damage to the Congressman had been done.

In March 2002 he was defeated in the Democrat primary for his district, a seat which he had held so comfortably in previous elections that he had started giving some of his campaign funds to charity.

The case against the media has merit; however there is also a good case for the defence. While television news programmes have a duty to report the issues of the day, they also must present them in a way which is accessible and interesting to the general public. If they did not do this, the public would get quickly bored and not watch the news at all. For those with a desire to see a more in-depth analysis of politics, coverage is available. CSPAN, for instance, broadcasts live sessions of Congress and reports on Congressional politics. Programmes such as *Nightline, Meet the Press* and *Face the Nation* provide a more detailed coverage of issues than the regular news programmes. Newspapers such as the *New York Times* and the *Washington Post* also provide a good level of political analysis. It can be argued that, while the media is guilty of sensationalism, in the case of Gary Condit, they pursued a valid story. While such scandals have nothing to do with the policies members of Congress advocate, they point to flaws in character and judgement. Candidates for Congress often make great of their strength of character in an attempt to win votes and once elected need to be trusted to use their judgement to the benefit of their constituents and the nation as a whole.

Interest groups

Interest groups (or pressure groups) are groups of individuals or organisations who band together in order to promote or defend their shared interests. The American political system provides numerous access points for anyone looking to influence policy. Groups can approach individual members of Congress, Congressional committees and staff, executive branch departments and agencies along with numerous state and local government institutions. The strategies groups use to influence Congress vary depending on their size and resources.

Insider strategies

Insider strategies involve direct contact between interest groups and members of Congress (or their staff). Those groups with sufficient resources will hire professional lobbying firms to contact lawmakers on their behalf. Professional lobbyists will have expert knowledge of how the legislative process works and who the key players are for any issue and will have developed relationships with members of Congress over time. Many lobbyists are former members of Congress or Congressional staffers. Worried about conflicts of interests, there is a legal 'cooling off period' which prevents Representatives and Senators from moving immediately from elected office to a lobbying firm. Small interest groups lobbying on their own can often find problems in gaining access to members, especially on major issues where there are many groups competing for their time. Groups can start to overcome this problem by establishing offices in Washington DC and building relationships over a period of time.

One of the biggest advantages interest groups hold is their knowledge of the issues they are concerned with. This expertise can be used in a number of ways: to try and persuade a member to vote in the required direction, to supply sympathetic members with evidence or arguments to use in support of their view, or to testify in front of a committee hearing.

Committee hearings are the most high profile of arenas where groups can put their arguments to Congress. There is some doubt, however, as to whether evidence put to the committee can actually change the minds of long-standing committee members. This was considered in chapter 3.

The most controversial aspect of interest groups' activities is the money donated to the campaign funds of sitting and prospective members of Congress. As discussed in chapter 2, despite interest groups being restricted by the Federal Election Campaign Act to donations of $5,000 per candidate per election, the amount of money received by all candidates has risen dramatically since the 1970s. In addition the rise in so-called 'soft money' donations to local political parties have increased interest groups' financial investment in the electoral process. The fear expressed by campaigning groups such as *Common Cause* and *The Center for Responsive Politics* is that a political system awash with financial contributions from businesses groups and other interests opens itself to the danger of corruption (see Appendix).

The loophole of soft money was finally regulated in 2002 when a bill co-sponsored by Republican Senator John McCain of Arizona passed Congress after a long struggle. McCain, had consistently advocated campaign finance reform after being caught in a scandal involving donations. In 1989, five Senators were accused of attempting to interfere with an investigation into the collapse of a Savings and Loan company owned by Charles Keating. It emerged that Keating, in total, had donated over $1 million to those Senators' campaign funds. After a lengthy investigation, the Senate criticised four of the Senators for poor judgement and reprimanded one, Senator Alan Cranston of California for 'improper and repugnant' conduct. The Senate concluded that Senators John

McCain and John Glenn had not been extensively involved.

This was not the first time the US Congress had been hit by scandal involving money. In 1980, in the 'ABSCAM' scandal, an FBI undercover operation brought charges of bribery against six Representatives and one Senator. All either resigned their seats or were defeated in the next election, except Congressman Michael J. 'Ozzie' Myers who was expelled from the House. In 1997 House Speaker Newt Gingrich was fined over $30,000 following charges of ethics violations and misleading the House over his use of funds from a non-profit organisation for political purposes. The scandal contributed to his early retirement from Speakership and ultimately from the House. The irony in the Gingrich scandal was that, in 1989, he had been at the forefront of a campaign which led to the resignation of Speaker Jim Wright following allegations of misuse of funds from book royalties.

For the most part, however, donations from interest groups are open and made within the law. Whether donations can 'buy' a member's vote is open for debate. While a donation of $5,000 is no small amount, it is only a fraction of the average total raised by members of Congress, especially for those running for the Senate. The first consideration of any member when deciding how to act or cast a vote will be the possible reaction of their constituents. In most circumstances, no amount of money from an interest group will persuade a member to vote or act in a way that would jeopardise their re-election. However, on issues which are not high profile, or which constituents have little interest in, there remains a question of to what extent money can sway votes. Academic studies do not agree; some suggest a link between donations and votes, others argue that no link exists at all.

In the majority of cases, however, money is not spent in an

attempt to change the view of members of Congress, instead it tends to flow from interest groups to members who are already sympathetic to their position. With this, groups are trying to achieve two things. Firstly, by donating money to the election campaigns of candidates who support their position, groups hope to facilitate the election of members sympathetic to their cause. Secondly, if that member is returned to Congress, groups hope that their financial investment will result in improved access. Donations are normally used as part of a wider lobbying strategy, with the money being used to increase the effectiveness of a group's arguments and persuasion.

For most groups, the money available for political donations is limited. This means that targeting the right members is crucial if the money is to be used effectively. It will be of little use to a group if their campaign contributions find their way to members who are publicly opposed to that group's point of view. Funds will also not be used efficiently if given to members who are unable or unwilling to make an impact in Congress on the donating group's key issue. Consequently, groups will often target members of Congress who sit on a committee with jurisdiction over the issue, especially those who have a track record of activity in the area of concern

Outsider strategies

Outsider strategies are those which groups use to put pressure on Congress and its members without working directly in Capitol Hill itself. Such strategies look to mobilise and demonstrate public support around their issue. The aim of outsider action is to suggest to members of Congress that their stand on the issue may have electoral consequences. Examples of such strategies can include organising demonstrations, letter writing campaigns or advertising in the media.

There is some question to how effective outsider strategies are in influencing the legislative process. It is argued that groups resort to such activities when, unlike, say, business groups, they do not have the resources or contacts to effectively lobby from within Congress. On Mothers' Day 2000, one of the largest public protests America had seen took place under the name 'The Million Mom March'. The March was a protest against gun violence and for legal controls on the possession of firearms. Over 750,000 people marched on the National Mall in Washington DC. Thousands also joined marches in towns and cities across the country. The demonstrations achieved maximum publicity for the cause of gun control, but had very little impact in terms of new legislation.

However, this assessment is not entirely fair. Research by Kay Schlozman and John Tierney suggests that rather than a last resort, public activity is the norm for a majority of interest groups. They estimated that over 80 per cent of groups engaged in grassroots lobbying and letter- writing campaigns, and one-third of groups placed adverts in the media.[2] These efforts are often used to supplement more direct lobbying. While change may not be achieved immediately, public campaigns can have the effect of keeping an issue on the political agenda. Throughout the 1950s and 1960s, civil rights demonstrations led by interest groups such as the National Association for the Advancement of Colored People (NAACP) made a huge impact on the national political scene. Television pictures of the brutality which occasionally greeted the marchers highlighted the issue further. These public displays were central to the debate which eventually led to the passage of the 1964 Civil Rights Act.

For most groups, such mass action is impossible to organise. Letter-writing campaigns or marches will be much more low key. The success of small group action will depend on how effectively they can target individual constituencies of members.

Is there a level playing field?

All interest groups are not equal; inevitably some will have larger financial resources, others will have greater public support. However, one question which has long been debated is that if a group is sufficiently resourced and organised to lobby Congress, will they find a level playing field? The arguments on this matter can be characterised by two extremes – *pluralism* and *elite theory*.

Pluralist group theory, expounded by such writers as Arthur Bentley and David Truman, views government as a neutral arbiter of competing interests.[3] Government has no preconceived position on any issue, but instead acts as the venue where interest groups can compete to influence policy. In the case of Congress, it will be the committees which provide the focus for competition between interests. Under the pluralist model, as problems arise, groups will mobilise in response. As one interest gets their way in terms of policy, others will mobilise in opposition, forming what are known as *policy subsystems*. If there is significant support for a point of view, this will be represented at government level. In this way, the battle between organised interests is a dynamic one which shifts and changes with political and social developments. An often quoted example of such mobilisation is the rise of the labour movement during the 1930s in response to hardships brought on by the Great Depression.

At the other end of the theoretic spectrum is elite theory. Under this model, government is a vested interest in itself, rather than some sort of neutral arbiter. Government is populated by types of people with similar backgrounds, views and values. A leading elite theorist, C. Wright Mills, writing in 1956, described those elected to Congress thus

> as social types . . . [they] are not representative of the rank and file citizens. They represent those who have been success-ful in entrepreneurial and professional endeavours. Older men, they are of the privileged white, native-born of native parents, Protestant Americans. They are college graduates and they are at least solid, upper-middle class in income and status. On average, they have had no experience of wage or lower salaried work. They are, in short, in and of the new and old upper classes of local society.[4]

As discussed in chapter 2, the background of members of Congress had become more diverse since Mills was writing. However, the accusation still remains that Washington estab-lishment is still dominated by a business-oriented upper class and their shared attitudes set the parameters for debate. Accordingly, groups representing big business will have a huge advantage over public interests. They will have greater contacts throughout Washington DC, better resources and share the beliefs and goals of most members of Congress.

One variant of elite theory is that which suggests that the policy process is dominated by *iron triangles* (briefly discussed in chapter 4). The three points of the triangle are the Con-gressional committee with jurisdiction over an issue, the department or agency with responsibility for executing the law and certain interested groups. The argument runs that each part of the triangle reaches consensus on the direction of policy and because of the dominance of the committee over the legislative process, dissenting voices are not allowed in. The most famous case of an iron triangle was suggested by President Eisenhower in his farewell speech, when he warned of the dangers of the 'military–industrial complex'. In this example, it is the Armed Services Committee of Congress (the members of which will often represent constituencies where the military is a major employer), the department of defense (or Pentagon) and groups such as arms manufacturers. All parts of this triangle have an interest in increasing spending on defense and have the ability to dominate the policy process, regardless of the impact of the policy on the economy or society as a whole.

Since the Republican Party took control of Congress in 1995, there have been accusations that business groups and others have received unprecedented access to the legislative process. The accusations were particularly directed at policy making on environmental and energy issues. Environmental groups complained that the very companies who were subject to environmental laws made by Congress were allowed to work closely with the Republican majority to rewrite legislation. One Republican Congressional aide admitted there was some truth to this, but argued that there was no conspiracy at work,

> [Environmental groups] brought that up as an issue and I think that is a bogus issue. They work with Democrats; Democrats are their allies and the environmentalists work very hard to get . . . Democrats elected. It should be no surprise that when the Democrats are writing a bill they would call in their friends and when the Republicans are writing a bill they are going to call in their friends. We [Republicans] talked to the environmentalists, they testified before our committees in, I think, fairly balanced hearings. But it shouldn't surprise anyone, unless they are really naive, that Republicans would be a little more solicitous of farmers' concerns or some business concerns. That is what the whole election is about.[5]

The reality of Congressional-interest group relations probably falls somewhere between the pluralist and elite models. The idea of iron triangles must be disputed. Hugh Heclo has argued that such tight 'subgovernments' have proved very difficult to maintain, and instead he suggests that more diverse *issue networks* have arisen. He accepts that certain groups with expert knowledge and shared values will work closely with committees and bureaucrats, but that the large number of participants will prevent any permanent consensus being reached.

While big business will have a major advantage in lobbying Congress through its resources, expertise and relationships in government, this does not mean that public-interest groups are doomed to failure. Ralph Nader, who ran as a Green Partry candidate for the presidency in 1996 and 2000, has shown how a public campaigner can have an effect. In 1965, Nader published a book entitled *Unsafe at any speed*, which exposed the poor safety standards which he claimed existed throughout the American car industry. Nader's campaign was highly influential in the passage of the 1966 National Traffic and Motor Vehicle Safety Act. Nader went on to lead campaigns on food safety and environmental issues. However, it can be argued that such success stories are the exception and that in the day-to-day business of lawmaking, small public-interest groups will struggle to make a major impact.

Summary

Media and interest groups have an impact on Congress. The media will influence how Congress is perceived by the public. The growth of television has led to accusations that the media, in search of entertainment and viewing figures, has trivialised politics, focusing on sensation rather than news. Interest groups try to influence Congress in a number of ways. Their tactics can be divided into outsider and insider strategies. The most controversial of strategies is the donation of money to members' campaigns. This has led to accusations of corruption, although the evidence for how far money can 'buy' votes is mixed. What is also of concern is that it can be argued that only the biggest and richest groups have a significant effect on the legislative process.

Appendix: top gun

In its bid to quash legislation that would respond to a rash of school shootings by strengthening the nation's gun laws, the National Rifle Association (NRA) outspent gun control advocates nearly 50–1 in campaign contributions to members of Congress in the first half of 1999. Newly filed records with the Federal Election Commission show the NRA contributed more than $270,000 from its political action committee to members of Congress between Jan. 1 and July 31, 1999, 81 percent to Republicans. During the same period, Handgun Control, a leading advocate for new gun laws, made $5,500 in PAC contributions, all to Democrats.

Such spending came during a period when Congress was wrestling with proposed legislation that included stronger regulations on gun shows and measures that would determine whether gun manufacturers could be held liable for damage caused by guns. The most contentious debate emerged after a spate of deadly school shootings, including the April massacre of 14 students and a teacher at Colorado's Columbine High School. Lawmakers, propelled by outrage over Columbine and rising gun violence, introduced several measures, including amendments to limit the number of handguns that a household could purchase each month.

Analysis of the NRA's political giving shows contributions to lawmakers were made alongside key events during the gun-control debate. During May, the NRA PAC contributed $23,550 to law-makers, almost all of which was given on May 6 – the same day Senate Democrats unveiled what would be the first of numerous gun-control policy packages on Capitol Hill. Among the recipients was Sen. Slate Gorton (R-Wash.), who received $1,000. Gorton is a longtime critic of proposed gun curbs, who would emerge as a prominent supporter of the NRA in the recent debate. 'We all know that there is no effective legislation we could pass that would comply with the First Amendment' Gorton told the Christian Science Monitor on May 6.

In a major defeat for the NRA just days later, the Senate narrowly rejected, then approved, a juvenile-justice bill that included controls on the import of gun ammunition as well as a mandatory three-business day check on the buyers of weapons sold at gun shows. The bill's passage marked the first time in more than five years that lawmakers had approved substantial gun-control legislation. In June, as the House prepared to take up its own version of the gun bill, the NRA nearly quadrupled its contributions to lawmakers. The NRA PAC reported giving $88,500 to lawmakers that month, with more than $80,000 going to House members. Seventy-four percent of the NRA contributions in June went to House Republicans.

On June 7, House Democrats and Republicans began crafting separate versions of a juvenile-justice bill that would be introduced later in the week. That same day, the NRA contributed $31,700 to lawmakers, including $1,000 to Rep. John Dingell (D-Mich.) and $2,500 to Rep. Bud Cramer (D-Ala.), two prominent Democrats who would join the Republicans in defeating the gun bill. Dingell, during the House debate, sponsored an amendment that would limit background checks at gun shows to 24 hours, after which the weapon could be sold to the buyer whether or not the check had been completed. Later, he urged conservative Democrats to vote against the entire gun bill, even though his amendment had been approved. 'There are sensible ways to ensure law-abiding citizens' rights to purchase firearms while forever closing the gun-show loophole,' Dingell told The Washington Times.

Gun control advocates, who viewed the House juvenile justice bill as too weak, united on June 17 with gun rights proponents, who viewed the bill as too strong, to defeat the measure. Within a week, the NRA gave $52,800 to lawmakers, nearly $16,000 of which went to House Democrats who voted against new gun curbs.

By Holly Bailey

Reproduced with the permission of The Center for Responsive Politics (www.opensecrets.org).

Notes

1 Center For Media And Public Affairs.
2 K. L. Schlozmand and J. T. Tierney, *Organized Interests and American Democracy* (New York: Harper & Row, 1986), p. 150.
3 A. Bentley, *The Process of Government* (San Antonio: Trinity University Press, 1949); D. B. Truman, *The Governmental Process* (New York: Alfred Knopf, 1951).
4 C. W. Mills, *The Power Elite* (Oxford: Oxford University Press, 1956), p. 248.
5 Interview conducted by author, 16/5/96, Washington DC.

9

Assessing the US Congress

I have wondered at times what the Ten Commandments would have looked like if Moses had run them through the US Congress. (President Ronald W. Reagan)

At first glance, while the nation of the United States of America has changed greatly since the Constitution was written in 1787, the political system has remained remarkably stable. The United States is still a federal system, with its government based on the separation of the executive, legislative and judicial powers. Congress, the legislative branch of the government, remains a bicameral body, with the differences between its two chambers based upon the principles laid down by the Founding Fathers. However, further investigation of the American political establishment at the beginning of the twenty-first century reveals some significant changes. The role of the federal government has been transformed; it now reaches into every area of American life requiring Congress to deal with issues as diverse as taxation, space exploration, gun control and the ethics of cloning. The presidency has claimed for itself a much greater part in the initiation of legislation than the Founding Fathers ever would have imagined. Congress has been forced to respond to this new challenge along with other changes such as the increase in interest-group activity, the importance of money within the political system, the development of mass communication and the establishment of primary elections as the first step towards securing a seat in the House of Representatives or Senate.

It is possible to argue that the way in which the Constitution has been able to adapt to such changes without the need for significant amendment, is a triumph for the American political structure. However, it could also be argued that many of the difficulties faced by the United States in the new century will not be solved easily using eighteenth-century institutions. Such a view resonates with President Reagan's famous assertion that the growth of federal power since 1933 has led to a situation where 'government is not the solution to our problem; government is the problem'.

For any student of the US Congress this is a difficult but important issue. It is also one which the American public has no consistent view on. Opinion polls in 1990 suggested that Congress was failing in its task; when the public was asked whether they approved of the way Congress was doing its job, the highest positive response rate gained in that year was 28 per cent, with 65 per cent disapproving and 7 per cent expressing no opinion.[1] It was to take until January 1999 for Congress's approval rating to reach over 50 per cent. In recent years, however, the poll results have been much more encouraging, with public approval hitting a high of 84 per cent in October of 2001. While this extraordinary high result can be attributed to the aftermath of the terrorist attacks on New York and Washington DC (the previous month produced an approval score of 42 per cent), since early 2000, Congress has been consistently receiving higher approval than disapproval ratings.

Opinion polls are a good snapshot of the public mood at one time, but as the results from November 2001 show, they can be influenced by a variety of factors. The problematic question of whether Congress 'works' is, though, an important one. This chapter will examine that question by considering some of the challenges faced by the modern Congress.

Gridlock

The term *gridlock* became popular in the 1980s. Originally used to describe standstill in New York City traffic jams, it was soon adopted by political journalists to refer to an inability by Congress and/or the President to enact new legislation, even if there was seemingly a majority in favour of action. The reasons for gridlock occurring in the political system are plentiful. The Founding Fathers must take their fair share of the blame (or credit, depending on your view). The system of checks and balances, designed to prevent the rise of a despotic government, can also make legislating a difficult task. With the agreement of the House, Senate and the President needed for a bill to become a law (the exception being when Congress overrides a presidential veto), any one of those bodies can prevent a law being enacted. The most extreme example of this in recent years was the stand-off between Congress and White House in 1995 over the budget which led to a government shutdown. Compromises between the branches of government are hard fought and often difficult to achieve.

It can be argued that such disagreements between the President and Congress have increased in recent years because of the tendency towards divided government – where different parties control the executive and legislative branches of government. Between 1969 and 2001, divided government was in place for all but six years. With different policy agendas being pursued by the White House and Congress, it is perhaps not surprising that gridlock occurs. However, this explanation is not enough by itself. Even when the same party has controlled both branches of government, this has not meant that the difficulties inherent in passing legislation have disappeared. Indeed, Democrat Presidents Carter and Clinton both faced problems with achieving their legislative goals even when the Democrats were in charge of Congress.

Congress itself can contribute to problems of gridlock. The gate-keeping function of Congressional committees provides a large barrier to action at the very beginning of the legislative process in both the House of Representatives and the Senate. Additionally, the lack of sanctions available to the party leaders to force members to behave or vote in a particular way make any form of party government near impossible. As Newt Gingrich discovered while attempting to pass the measures included in the *Contract with America*, the bicameral structure of Congress can cause problems. Even when one chamber votes in favour of legislation, there is no guarantee that their colleagues on the other side of Congress will do likewise.

Interest groups have also been blamed for Congressional inaction. Advocates of healthcare reform regularly point to the money donated to Congressional candidates by health insurance companies as a major factor in Congress's failure to pass comprehensive healthcare legislation. The same arguments are made by those frustrated by the reluctance of Congress to pass further restrictions on the ownership of guns. The contention is that the nature of the legislative process makes it easy for members to block the progress of new laws, especially by those on the appropriate committee, without drawing public attention to their actions. Consequently, while interest groups may find it difficult to persuade Congress to pass new laws, they are far more successful in using their influence to prevent the passage of legislation.

While gridlock has on occasions been a feature in modern American Government, the extent of the problem should not be overstated. In recent periods of divided government, pieces of major legislation have been successfully passed, often through compromise between Congress and the presidency. To characterise gridlock as a constant feature of the US political system would be just as erroneous as to deny that it exists at all. Even when gridlock does prevent Congress from passing legislation, this does not automatically lead to the conclusion that it is failing in its job as the federal legislature. It could be argued that the point of the checks and balances is to ensure that laws are not made casually; that it is right that it is easier to block a law than to pass one. This is partly a subjective matter, as former Senate Republican leader and Presidential nominee Bob Dole commented, 'if you're against something you'd better hope there is a little gridlock'. It is also a function of the designs of the Founding Fathers and their concern to prevent an overpowerful government. There is a case to be made that the federal system was designed to make it difficult to pass legislation and that gridlock is evidence that the government is working as it should.

The making of coherent policy

One further accusation against Congress is that it is unable of passing a coherent policy programme in the interests of the national good. This was touched on in chapter 2. This argument is a function of two features of Congress: the re-election impulse of members and the power of the committee. With members focused throughout their term of office on the need for re-election, the interests and preferences of their constituents will be a priority. Representatives and Senators will behave and take positions in order to benefit their voters and, if possible, ensure that the benefits of legislation are targeted at their constituency. The committee system allows members to specialise in issues of concern or potential benefit to their constituents and exercise a great deal of influence over those areas of policy due to the position of the committee in the legislative process. The result of this, critics argue, is a system of policy making which is directed at parochial concerns rather than any greater national need.

As argued before, the whole notion of 'the national good' is a subjective one. When subsidies for farmers are passed by the Agriculture Committee or funds for a building project benefit the constituency of a member of the Public Works Committee, Congress is accused of legislating in a parochial manner. Those communities who benefited from such Congressional action would, no doubt, contend that the legislation was not only necessary but was evidence of Congress acting in the national interest. It can also be argued that Congress was established as a representative body, and would be failing in its task if members did not work for the benefits of their constituents.

Challenges for the twenty-first century

One further question to be considered is whether the structure of the legislative process makes Congress able to tackle the issues that will emerge in the new century. It could be argued that a system which appears to make inaction easy to achieve will always be better at sustaining the status quo than producing innovative programmes. Congressional policy making can often be characterised as incremental. Programmes are introduced and amended over time as feedback is received about the successes and failures. It is far easier for Congress as a whole and members individually to look to amend existing policies than it is to embark on whole new programmes. This is consistent with the view of Congress as one where power is decentralised, with many hurdles for legislation to cross and dominated by members with re-election uppermost in their minds. However, this can create a problem when entirely new challenges arise or when it becomes clear that the existing approach to a problem is fundamentally inadequate.

Budget deficit

At the heart of the budget stand-off between President Clinton and the Republican-controlled Congress was the issue of the federal budget deficit. The growth of government spending throughout the post-war period had led to small budget deficits being reported throughout the 1950s and 1960s. The economic picture worsened in the 1970s and the issue of the deficit became prominent in the 1980 presidential election. The election in 1980 of Ronald Reagan with a Republican majority in the Senate, promised for some the opportunity for a more fiscally conservative approach to spending. However, if their policy was to bring the budget back into surplus, they failed completely. By the time Reagan left office in 1989, the deficit had reached $200 billion. Critics of the President argued that his policy of cutting taxes while at the same time pushing for large increases in defence spending caused the national debt to escalate. Reagan and his supporters aimed their fire at the inability of the US Congress to relinquish their attachment to spending on pork barrel projects and inefficient programmes. Congressional attempts to pass legislation which would force spending down (most notably the 1987 Gramm-Rudman-Hollings Act) proved ineffective and by the time of the 1992 presidential election the budget deficit was only a little short of $300 billion.

The state of the economy was to dominate the 1992 election and although some progress was made, when the Republicans took over control of Congress in 1995, the deficit was still in excess of $150 billion. Determined to bring the budget into surplus, the Republican majority proposed sweeping cuts in social spending which were to bring Congress into conflict with the Clinton White House and lead to the stand-off which saw the government shutdown for a short period in late 1995. There was even an unsuccessful attempt by Congress to amend the Constitution to force future lawmakers to maintain a balanced budget. However, once again the problem of reducing government outlays and protecting valuable social programmes prevented the US Government from finding a solution to the problem.

Compromise was eventually reached between President Clinton and Congress and in 1998 the Office of Management and Budget reported a surplus for the first time since 1969. The problem, though, has not gone away. A combination of Congress passing the deep tax cuts proposed by President George W. Bush and increases in defence and other spending (partially in a response to the terrorist attacks of 2001, although not exclusively) will lead to budget deficits in 2002, 2003 and 2004.

Social security

The problem of the budget deficit has an impact on another emerging issue – the future of social security. Through a

programme established in 1935, all working Americans contribute through payroll taxes to a fund which is used to
support retired and disabled citizens and their dependants.
The problem which is faced by the government is that due to
population growth and longer life expectancy, it is projected
that by 2016, benefits will begin outpacing revenues, and by
2038 the surplus will be exhausted entirely.

The solution to this problem is not clear and has caused a
certain amount of controversy. Democrats in particular argue
that the current system is essentially sound and that only
incremental change is necessary. Others, including President
George W. Bush are pushing for more fundamental reform.
One particular proposal is to create individual social security
accounts in which payroll taxes would be invested to provide
for future payments. Critics of the scheme argue that invest-
ing revenue in stocks could prove risky and that the use of
individual accounts would mean a decrease in the level of payments to cover transaction charges.

The future of social security is the sort of problem that
Congress must address successfully if it is to be considered an
effective legislature. If a fundamentally new approach is
indeed necessary, then Congress must prove the stereotype of
a legislature dominated by local interests which favours
gradual change wrong. As with any law-making body, it must
ultimately be judged on its success in tackling the problems
which its society faces.

Summary

Assessing whether Congress 'works' is no easy task. It is
difficult to decide on the criteria by which it should be
judged. Gridlock is often quoted as evidence of the political

establishment malfunctioning, however, it could also be argued that the system was designed to make it difficult for laws to be passed. On any one issue, it is a matter of opinion whether the passage of a new law is the desirable course of action. Similarly, while accusations of parochialism are frequently levelled at Congress, it must also function as a representative body and any judgement of what is in the national interest is bound to be subjective. The appropriate criteria with which to judge Congress is perhaps how effectively it can address the challenges which will emerge in the new century.

Notes

1 All figures taken form Gallup polls conducted from October 1990 to June 2002.

Select bibliography

Arnold, R. D. *The Logic of Congressional Action* (New Haven: Yale University Press, 1990)

Bailey, C. J. *The US Congress* (Oxford: Basil Blackwell, 1989)

Bentley, A. *The Process of Government* (San Antonio: Trinity University Press, 1949)

Boller Jr., P. F. *Congressional Anecdotes* (Oxford: Oxford University Press, 1991)

Cigler, A. J. and B. A. Loomis (eds.), *Interest Group Politics* (3rd Edition, Washington DC: CQ Press, 1991)

Cox, G. W. and M. D. McCubbins, *Legislative Leviathan: Party Government in the House* (Berkeley: University of California, 1993)

Davidson, R. H. *The Postreform Congress* (New York: St. Martin's Press, 1992)

Davidson, R. H. and W. J. Oleszek, *Congress and Its Members* (2nd Edition, Washington DC: CQ Press, 1985)

Deering, C. J. and S. S. Smith, *Committees in Congress* (Washington DC: CQ Press, 1984)

Dodd, L. and B. I. Oppenheimer (eds.), *Congress Reconsidered* (5th Edition, Washington DC: CQ Press, 1993)

Fenno Jr., R. F. *Congressmen in Committees* (Boston: Little Brown, 1973)

Fenno, R. F. *Learning to Govern: An Institutional View of the 104th Congress* (Washington DC: Brookings Institution Press, 1997)

Fiorina, M. *Divided Government* (Boston Allyn & Bacon, 1996)

Foley, M. and J. E. Owens, *Congress and the Presidency: Institutional Politics in a Separated System* (Manchester: Manchester University Press, 1996)

Hall, R. L. *Participation in Congress* (New Haven and London: Yale

University Press, 1996)

Kingdon, J. W. *Congressmen's Voting Decisions* (3rd Edition, Ann Arbour: University of Michigan Press, 1989)

Krehbiel, K. *Information and Legislative Organization* (Ann Arbor: University of Michigan Press, 1991)

Mayhew, D. R. *Congress: The Electoral Connection* (New Haven: Yale University Press, 1974)

Mayhew, D. R. *Divided We Govern: Party Control, Lawmaking and Investigations, 1946–1990.* (New Haven: Yale University Press, 1991)

McSweeney, D. and J. E. Owens (eds.), *The Republican Takeover of Congress* (London: McMillan Press, 1998)

Mills, C. W. *The Power Elite* (Oxford: Oxford University Press, 1956)

O'Neil, T. *All Politics is Local* (Holbrook MA: Bob Adams Inc., 1994)

Rieselbach, L. N. *Congressional Politics* (Oxford: Westview Press, 1995)

Smith, S. S. *The American Congress* (Boston: Houghton Mifflin, 1999)

Truman, D. B. *The Governmental Process* (New York: Alfred Knopf, 1951)

Wilson, W. *Congressional Government* (New York: Meridian, 1956)

Index

ABSCAM scandal 150
Abzug, Bella 115–16
African American
    representation of 40–2
    voters 31
amendments 98, 109, 111–13,
    116–18
Armey, Richard *89*, 103
Articles of Confederation 5–7

Bentley, Arthur 153
Bernstein, Carl 145
Bill of Rights 12
budget
    budget deficit 166–7
    budget dispute (1995) 135–8,
        162, 165–7
    and Ronald Reagan 132–3
bundling 30
Bush, George W. *33*, 129, *135*,
    167–8

campaign finance 26–31,
    149–51
    reform *81*, 118, 149

candidate-centred campaigning
    17–20
Cannon, 'Uncle' Joe 90
Capra, Frank 110
Carter, Jimmy *33*, *34*, 129, *135*
    163
case work 48–9
checks and balances 7–8,
    10–11, 121–7, 162–4
Chomsky, Noam 145–6
Civil Rights Act (1964) 80,
    96–7, 112, 152
Clinton, Bill *33*, *34*, 35, 37, 85,
    130–2, *135*
    and government shutdown
        135–8, 166–7
    impeachment of 54–7, 124–7
Clinton, Hillary 26–7, 125,
    131–2
cloture 111
committees *64*
    appointment to 47–8, 70–1,
        88, 90
    bias within 71–5
    classification of *72*

committees (*cont.*)
  committee chair 75–6
  committee government 61
  committee of the whole 107
  control of 79–82
  democrat reforms 80–3
  distributive theory of 73
  gate-keeping 63–5, 69
  hearings 66–8, 148–9
  informational theory of 74–5
  iron-triangles 85, 154–6
  log-rolling 77–8
  mark-up 68–9
  oversight 121
  policy bias 71–5
  pork barrel and 50–1
  power of 76–9, 115
  power within 75–6
  proxy voting in 75, 84
  ranking minority member 52,
    75, 83, 107
  referral to 88, 96–7
  republican reforms 82–4
  seniority 52, 96
  types of 62–3
  unity within 78–9
Condit, Gary 146–7
conference committees 99–100,
    116–18
constituency service *see case
    work*
Constitution of the United
    States 6–8, 55, 82, 96
  amendments to 10, 12, 58
  Congress in 8–12
continuing resolution 136
Contract with America 16–17,

35–8, 57, 83, 95, 101–3,
    163
Corzine, Jon 26, *28*
Cranston, Alan 149
C-SPAN 147

Daschle, Thomas *89*, 103
Declaration of Independence 4
Dirksen, Everette *140–2*
discharge petition 79–80, *81*
divided government 138–9,
    162–3
Dole, Bob 16, 95, 138, 164

Eisenhower, Dwight D. *33, 34,
    135*
  military-industrial complex
    and 85, 154–5
electoral connection 43–5
Everett, Terry 73

Federal Election Campaign Act
    29
federalism 7
Feingold, Russ 31
Fenno, Richard 44–5
filibuster 109–11
floor debates 105–16
Foley, Thomas 35
foreign policy 122–4
franking privilege 24–5
French Indian War 3
Furse, Elizabeth 59

gate-keeping see under
    committees
Gephardt, Richard *89*, 103

Gingrich, Newt 16–17, 82–4,
    89, 90, *95–6*, 101–2,
    136–8, 150, 163
Gladstone, William 1
Glenn, John 150
Gorsuch, Anne 121
gridlock 162–4

healthcare 35–6, 69, 85, 131–2,
    137–9, 163
Heclo, Hugh 85, 156
House Rules Committee 98

impeachment 11, 54–7, 124–7
incumbency advantages 24–8,
    30
interest groups
    elite theory 153–6
    insider strategies 148–51
    outsider strategies 151–3
    pluralism 153–4
iron-triangles see under
    committees

Jefferson, Thomas 4, *134*
Jeffords, Jim 87–8, 129
Johnson, Andrew 125, *134*
Johnson, Lyndon B. *33*, *34*,
    123, 129, *135*, 140–2
Johnson treatment 94–5

Keating, Charles 149–50
Kennedy, John F. *33*, *34*, *135*,
    144
Krehbiel, Keith 74, 77

Lazio, Rick 26–7

leadership styles
    party leaders 94–6
    presidential 128–33
Lewinsky, Monica 54–5, 124
Locke, John 4, *5*
Long, Huey P. 111

Mayhew, David 43–4, 139
McCain, John 31, 149–50
media 143–7
Meehan, Martin *59*
Metcalf, Jack *59*
military-industrial complex *see
    under* Eisenhower
    Dwight D.
Million Mom March 152
Mills, C. Wright 154
money *see* campaign finance
morning business 106
morning hour 106
multiple referral 97
Myers, M. J., 'Ozzie' 150

Nader, Ralph 156
National Association for the
    Advancement of Colored
    People (NAACP) 152
National Rifle Association
    (NRA) *157–9*
Nethercutt, George *59*
Neustadt, Richard 128
New Deal *see under* Roosevelt
    Franklin D.
New York Times 144
Nixon, Richard M. *33*, *34*,
    135, 123
    Watergate 14, 63, 144–5

occupations of members of
    Congress 40–3, *41*
O'Neil, Tip 2, 25, 32
opinion polls *23*, 36, 127, 161
oversight 120–7

parties 87–104
    government 101–3
    identification 20, 22, *23*, 25
    leaders 88–96
    unity 100–1
Perot, H. Ross 130
Pledge of Allegiance 106
policy bias see under
    committees
policy specialisation 46–8
political action committees
    29–30
political capital 130–3
pork barrel see under
    committees
President of the United States
    coat-tails 32, *33*
    legislative leadership 13–14,
        127–33
    veto 10–11, 102, 127, 139,
        133–8, *134–5*
President pro tempore 109
primary elections 19–20, 24

quorum 106–7, 110

Rayburn, Sam 90
Reagan, Ronald *33, 34,*
        129–30, 132–3, *135,*
        160–1, 166
    Iran-Contra 121–2

Rhenquist, William 124
Ribicoff, Abe *140–2*
Roosevelt, Franklin D. *134,*
    144
    New Deal 13–14, 101,
        127–8
Roosevelt, Theodore 13, 127,
    134
rule 107–9, *108*

seniority see under committees
separation of powers 7–8, 101,
    120, 160
Smith, Howard 112
social security 167–8
soft money 30–1, *81*, 149
Speaker of the House 88–90
    referral 96–7
    see also Gingrich, N.
split-ticket voting 32, 139
staff 24, 49, 53, 75, 82–3
Stamp Act (1765), 3
Starr, Kenneth *55*, 126
subcommittees 65–6
    subcommittee bill of rights
        82
Sugar Act (1764) 3
sunshine rules 82
Supreme Court 30, 58, 102,
    120

term limits 57–9
Thurmond, Strom 110
Truman, David 153

unanimous consent agreements
    99, 109

United States of America,
    foundation of 1–7
USA Today 144

Vice-President of the United
    States 109
Vietnam War 14, 122–3
voting in Congress
    113–15

War Powers Act (1973) 123
Washington Post 144–5
Watergate *see under* Nixon,
    Richard M.
Whitewater 54, 125
Wilson, Woodrow 13, 61, 82,
    127, *134*
Woodward, Bob 145
Wright, Jim 150